Instru____

LET AUGMENTED REA____

With your smartphone ____ ____ can use the
Hasmark AR app to invoke the augmented reality
experience to literally read outside the book.

1. Download the **Hasmark app** from the **Apple App Store** or **Google Play**

2. Open and select the option

3. Point your lens at the full image with the and enjoy the augmented reality experience.

Go ahead and try it right now with the cover of this book.

Once the content begins, click the '**Lock**' icon to lock the content onto your phone.

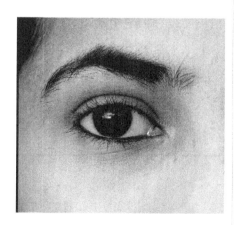

ENDORSEMENTS

"Angelica's story is one of pure authenticity and truth. There is no "hiding out" or making things sound good. It is a well written, captivating, honest documentation of a life well lived and very well described. Angelica has dealt with some of the hardest situations and circumstances, and has come out the other side committed to making a profound difference for humanity." I am proud to know Angelica and be her friend!"

Juli Hall, Founder,
Cherish Our Children Inc. (COCI)

"To share your truths is a bold move. Angelica Robles courageously shares her life story with us all. *Through These Brown Eyes* is a real-life experience that is undeniably raw, undeniably human."

—Peggy McColl,
New York Times bestselling author

"A book of profound impact and great importance, *Through These Brown Eyes* is the compelling story of Angelica Robles. Landing on her own two feet despite all that has been thrown her way, Angelica leaves her reader enlightened and in awe of her unmatched resilience."

—Judy O'Beirn,
President of Hasmark Publishing International

"This book fulfills the 4 Es rating system. It's Engaging, Emotional, Exciting, and full of Empathy! This is the sign of a good book, and a must read!"

—Brian Sebastian,
Movie Reviews and More

"Every now and then in this life, you're introduced to someone whose story really fascinates you. For me, that person is Angelica Robles. We were introduced by the amazing Lewis Senior, whose work I have revered for many years since I read his book *At the end of the Day* and discovered my own E-colors Personality style through his online platform. Angelica came into my life as a Yellow/Red, basically the female equivalent of my E-colors, and although I had taken the music path and she had taken another, I recognized and enjoyed the similarities immediately. As part of the promo work I was doing for my own book *Life Remixed*, I interviewed Angelica on my YouTube show *Straight Talking*. A bond was formed immediately and as a Life Coach what I loved most about her was that when I challenged her to write her own story down, she took me literally and did it in just a few short weeks! A woman of action you might say! What you'll find in these pages is a life well lived, a life scrutinised, a life under continual personal development, a life of purpose, and an ever-evolving journey. This book will inspire you to take action towards your goals and to enjoy achieving them consistently. Well done, Angelica! I'm looking forward to the movie! :)"

—Mark Wilkinson,
International Bestselling and
award-winning Author of *Life Remixed*

Through these these brown eyes

ANGELICA ROBLES

Hasmark
PUBLISHING
INTERNATIONAL

Cover Design: Anne Karklins | anne@hasmarkpublishing.com
Book Design: AmitDey | amit@hasmarkpublishing.com

ISBN 13: 978-1-77482-027-8
ISBN 10: 1774820277

Hasmark
PUBLISHING
INTERNATIONAL

DISCLAIMER

This book is based on true events. Some of the names in this book have been changed to protect the identity of the individuals.

PURPOSE OF
THROUGH THESE BROWN EYES

The purposes of this book are:

- To have you look into your heart and let go of any past fragments that you continue to drag along.
- To have you let go of past experiences that hinder your full potential and future growth.
- To have you be forgiving of your past, and of the people who have hurt you; be able to have grace and compassion for them and yourself.
- To have you honor the struggle and clear your mind of the fears that have made you a prisoner of your own thoughts.
- To allow yourself to feel all the emotions life brings, and to evolve in a way that you are limitless, unstoppable, and extraordinary.
- To have you get to a place where your perspective is clear, with nothing hindering your growth.

DEDICATION

To my gorgeous children on Earth, Belén and Zion, my most precious gifts from God. My all, my being, my motivation to continue to be a better mother and human being are these magnificent little souls.

TABLE OF CONTENTS

FOREWORD

by Lewis Senior,
CEO and Co-founder of Equilibria

There is a common expression that goes like this: "There are three versions of the truth: my version of the truth, your version of the truth, and the truth."

Angelica's book, written with such raw intensity, brings home to me just how real each event in her life has been lived. Her story spills off the pages as being *la verdad*, the truth, with no punches pulled. I have just finished reading the draft over several hours and was intrigued from cover to cover. Some elements I was aware of, and others were new to me.

I remain thankful that for whatever reason I have had the privilege of knowing Angelica at several junctures in her life, and now more than ever, as you will understand as you read on.

Angelica is a remarkable human being. She lights up any room on entry, and whichever facet of her life she is talking about, it's certainly never boring!

I met Angelica on a Friday afternoon several years ago sitting in the gallery at a board meeting for Cherish Our Children Inc. (COCI). I had requested the opportunity to attend, as I was keen to learn how a non-profit board operated as we in Equilibria were about to launch E-Colors in Education.

During a break, having spent a few minutes talking to Angelica, she sparked so much passion and energy about her commitment to raising funds for COCI that I returned the next day, and agreed to becoming a "pillar" for their organization with a three-year significant contribution. It also gave me the opportunity to share a little of what we are about on Equilibria. Immediately after I finished, Angelica told me that she wanted to be part of what we bring to the world through our personality diversity technology called E-Colors.

Not long after that, Angelica came to join us, having put to one side her work for other agencies. Angelica spent a couple of years with us and brought so much to us in Equilibria, our clients and friends. For all who know her, and for those of you reading this book, you will realize that Angelica does nothing by halves—if she's "in" she's "all-in" and her time with us was no different.

After leaving Equilibria to return to her work in investigation and interrogation, we kept in touch and she has always been a wonderful participant and advocate of our work through many different events over the years.

Through these Brown Eyes describes so many experiences and hard-learned life lessons that will leave you wondering just how Angelica has not only coped, but actually survived and flourished at times when others may have decided to throw in the towel. Frankly, I have nothing but admiration, respect, and appreciation for Angelica, and once you have read this book in its entirety you too will certainly not be left without some degree of awe and empathy for her life's trials and tribulations.

In late 2020, I contacted Angelica to see if she would be interested in being interviewed by our business associate in London, Mark Wilkinson, who had just written his own book called *Life Remixed* and had a streaming program called *Straight Talking*. I thought Angelica would make a great guest, so I put them in touch.

As Angelica told Mark some of her story, he suggested she consider writing a book. He put her in touch with his publishers . . . and here I am in March 2021, writing her foreword having already read her amazing story, her truth—the truth!

The impact of her book has created a situation that is both revealing, stunning, and life changing. Read on, and you will see for yourself.

Angelica, you own a very special place in my mind and heart. Thank you for allowing me into your world.

Un abrazo fuerte,

Lewis
CEO Equilibria,
Equilibria.com

ABOUT LEWIS SENIOR

(Yellow/Red)
Equilibria
#intentionalceo

Lewis Senior is a world-renowned intentional leadership and performance coach. Lewis co-founded Equilibria in 2004 after beginning to use personality diversity as a way to help those working on offshore drilling rigs minimize the risk of getting hurt or hurting others. "What we discovered was that these people were highly trained and skilled, but they often were not making smart decisions because their personalities were causing them to act and react in ways that reduced their ability to perform," says Lewis.

As a personality diversity expert, Lewis's proprietary methods to deliver meaningful change using personality as a common language are accepted and used by corporations and educational systems, as well as sports and non-profit organizations worldwide. More than 1.2 million individuals use Equilibria's approach to generate personal and professional success. The system has at its cornerstone a Personality Diversity Indicator. This simple tool uses colors (Red, Yellow, Blue, and Green) to heighten the awareness of self, team, and others.

Knowing your basic personality patterns and communication style are just the beginning, says Lewis. It's learning how to manage behavioral tendencies through Personal Intervention that truly makes the difference. My top color, Yellow, means that I am fast-paced and people-oriented. My energy comes from engaging with others. It also means that I often need to slow down and remember that not everyone acts and reacts in the same manner that I do. I constantly work on my listening skills, understanding that each of us brings a different valuable perspective to any endeavor.

Lewis knows firsthand about intentional self-management—the ability to move from a knee-jerk reaction to a conscious response when communicating with others. He co-authored an award-winning memoir, *At the End of the Day*, with his daughter Laura to recount their relationship struggles as she was coming of age. Today, their relationship is better than ever. In fact, not only is Lewis close to both of his children, but they, too, now play important management roles at Equilibria.

CHAPTER 1

THE BEGINNING

I began to feel weak, my vision became blurry, and a darkness overtook me. After four months of endless work, typing reports into the early hours of the morning and traveling nonstop, I finally hit a wall. I found myself in the ER hooked up to an IV. I had been vomiting violently because of serious stomach issues. This was my crash and burn. I had made a lot of money in my career, but my health had taken a hit as a result. I was fifty pounds overweight, depressed, overworked, and exhausted. I had fully depleted all of my electrolytes, and my body was shutting down. No one can ever tell you what the "crash and burn" is going to be like—you have to experience it for yourself. It was April of 2019, and I was in Austin, Texas, working numerous national security investigations when my crash and burn began. Had everything that had happened in my life led up to this moment?

I was the outcome of a birthday night of passion between my parents. In other words, I was totally unplanned. But as my mother used to say, "When you lay with a man, the possibility of a child is evident." The third and last child of the Robles bunch, I was born on a Sunday during a typically cold and gloomy Chicago fall afternoon. My parents, both in their twenties, first met at a bar in the city of my birth. My dad was quietly sitting at the bar (in his seventies-era bell bottoms, I am sure) when my gorgeous, tall, long-legged, mermaid-haired mother purposely bumped into him so he would turn around and look at her.

When I was born in 1982, my parents decided to move to Guadalajara, Mexico, so I lived the first six years of my life there. At first, I was very quiet and well-behaved . . . nothing like the inquisitive, questioning, and rebellious child I eventually became. The family—my parents, my brother Eddie, my sister Natalie, and I—lived in Colonia San Rafael on Handador La Costeña street in a small but beautiful yellow stucco house. Two towering pine trees out front made our house look chic. It was a cozy, two-story, three-bedroom home with two courtyards. For a few years, my maternal grandparents lived on the second floor of our home. For as long as I could remember, whenever it rained on our wide dirt road, an intoxicating smell of wet earth filled the air. I loved this smell; it reminded me of home. Later, this dirt road would be paved.

My mother never went to college or university, but her drive and impeccable work ethic are something all three of her children inherited. She was a stay-at-home mom with many passions in her life, which included cooking, dancing, and singing.

She has been cooking amazing and delectable food for as long as I can remember. The variety of food she introduced to us expanded our palates, and the smells of our home were as eclectic as one could ever imagine. The aroma of rum chocolate cake would fill the air, combined with *picadillo*—a ground beef, carrot, and pea Mexican stew with fluffy homemade *bisquetes* (biscuits). We even ate octopus, and especially loved those tentacles. My mother was very stringent with our food consumption, however, and we ate no junk food of any kind growing up. In fact, we didn't know what fast food was until we moved back to the U.S.

Growing up, music was a big part of our lives. My mother still sings gorgeously and can dance up a storm, even while jumping rope. The walls of our home were filled with sounds of the Sonora Santanera, a Mexican orchestra known for playing tropical music, and Elvis Presley. To this day, I can sing every single song from both Sonora and Elvis. Even without understanding the English lyrics, we would sing along to Elvis fluently. My mother had an eternal crush on The King, and his ever-quivering lip.

My father was born in a small town in Jalisco, Amacueca. Most of my father's family still reside there and own most of the local stores. My father was a locksmith and owned his own small business in Colonia Yáñez. Masterful with locks, my father was a hard worker and took house calls. If you got locked out—or locked in for that matter—my father was the person you called. His business thrived, and we lived a comfortable, yet humble, life. He drove a red 1975 Volkswagen Beetle and later, a cool beige and grey 1988 Dodge Ram station wagon. My father has had many odd job over the years, but being a locksmith really brought him joy. He has always been a funny and loving man. He worked long hours, but he always gave us his time. He still loves helping people and being of service. He sees the good in everyone. I get these qualities from my father.

When my maternal grandfather Ricardo and grandmother Guadalupe lived on the second floor of our home, every Sunday my grandfather would call us up for *Domingo*, or Sunday allowance. It was usually a peso, or even better, a chocolate bar. My maternal great-grandmother, Alta Gracia (we called her Altita), lived in a home in the town of San Luis Potosí where my mother grew up. San Luis Potosi is not far from Guadalajara. My great-grandmother and I shared the same birthday, and she lived to be ninety-five years old. She was born in 1910 and passed in 2005. My great-grandmother was powerful, loving, interesting and a seamstress extraordinaire. I have fond memories of us visiting with her, and of her showing us so much love. She would feed us until we exploded. During the Second French Intervention in Mexico in the 1860s, rumor has it that my great-great grandmother had an affair with a French soldier and became pregnant with my great-grandmother. My grandmother had curly red hair, which was a French-inherited trait. This red hair was then passed down to my mother's side of the family. These are the juicy stories that make family histories interesting.

Altita gifted us a thirty-six-year-old Amazon parrot. We called this parrot Lorito, which means "little parrot." Lorito used to sing, dance, and cry just like us. He was fun, and he liked my father most of all. When we moved to the United States, Lorito stayed behind with neighbors. We later found out that he was actually a she, and had laid an egg. After we abandoned Lorito, she eventually died. Parrots grow remarkably close to their owners and are known to die after their owners either abandon them or die.

Thanks to Lorito, the Robles kids always loved birds. My sister got two adorable baby geese for her birthday one year. We considered them pets, although I don't think we ever named them. These geese grew quickly, and were very loud. One day the geese were squawking their heads off, and the next day they were gone. My parents told us they had flown away. Years later, our parents told us the truth. My brother's godfather, Don Ernesto, who lived in the next block, came over to the house and slaughtered the geese. He cut their heads off with a machete, plucked them, and his wife Norma cooked them for *mole*. We later all ate the mole with our pet geese as the main ingredient.

My brother, Eddie, is six years older than I am. My sister, Natalie, is two years older than I am. Together, we got to experience middle-class Mexican life. We went to San Rafael Private School, which was run by the most austere Catholic nuns you can imagine. The school had a long black picket fence that ran across its entire front site. My mother, with her practiced hustler methods, convinced the harsh nuns to allow my three-year-old self to be admitted to kindergarten. These nuns meant business, but with some convincing—and a "donation"—they allowed me to join the school. I, by no means, was a fan of theirs and would often sneak out of kindergarten to join my sister in her class. Since my mother had paid the nuns, they allowed it to happen. These nuns exemplified the stringency of old-school Mexican Catholic private schools. They had long, hard yardsticks that they would use to slam on your desks, slap your hands, or even worse—your bottom. The nuns would line us up before school, check our nails for dirt, and our socks and skirts for length. If you were not up to their standards, they would smack your hands in front of everyone. But the most excruciating experience of all was having to turn around, pull your pants down and bare your bottom to receive a beating. This was the norm. Luckily for me, I never got a ruler to the hand, desk, or bottom.

I loved Christmas in our neighborhood. If you have never experienced a true Mexican Christmas season, you must. We had *posadas* every week where someone different hosted a party, prayed, brought out a baby Jesus, and provided awesome snacks. We feasted on *churros*, giant *conchas*, Mexican donuts, and *buñuelos*—giant fried sweet elephant ears. On Christmas Eve, everyone would come out to the street and bring their potluck dishes and piñatas. As a child, having over thirty pinatas to break was a dream! Can you imagine the amount of food and Mexican candy we indulged in? To this day, the Christmas season is one of my favorite Mexican memories.

I enjoyed playing with my sister and the other neighborhood kids. Our *colonia,* or block, had about six houses. Our best friend Maria lived across the street. It was not really a street, but more like a giant dirt road. Our neighbors to the right had six boys, and our elderly neighbor, also to the right, Don Aurelio, was a lonely, bitter, ball collector. When the balls that we played with became lost in his yard, they were never to be seen again. When we gathered the courage to knock on his door to ask for our balls, he would only look at us with his piercing eyes. He never returned our balls. As children, we were terrified of Don Aurelio. But looking back, I realize that he simply did not want to be bothered by the children in the neighborhood.

A corner store sat at the end of our block, and Don Pete, the owner, was a kind and gentle man. He sold soda in a bag. It might sound weird to kids today, but an orange soda in a plastic bag with a straw sticking out the top was a treat for us. Don Pete rode his bike from home to work. Many people rode bikes in those days. In fact, one day I was struck by one. All I can remember is that I didn't need to go to the emergency room. On the surface, our block might have seemed fun, full of laughter and neighborly love. But that was far from the truth.

One day as we played hide-and-seek, one of Maria's older brothers found me in my hiding spot, which happened to be the corner of a room in Maria's house. He said to me, "I found you. Did you think I wouldn't find you?" I remember these words as though the ordeal happened yesterday. He came close to me, close to my face, my tiny three-year-old body, and put his hands down my pants. He touched my privates, and rubbed his hands all over my tiny body. As a three-year-old, I was smaller than most (I grew up to be only five feet, three inches as an adult). I was scared, frozen, ashamed, and mortified. Even at three years old, I knew this behavior was wrong. He told me that if I told anyone about what he had done, he would do it again. I ran to my house and never told anyone until I was seventeen years old and in therapy for major depression. This incident not only changed my mindset about trust, but it also robbed my innocent mind of the joy of playing hide-and-seek. I became increasingly quiet and shy. Later, I found out that he had done the same thing to other neighborhood girls, and possibly even to his own sister.

I loved playing with my sister; she was older and always had the best ideas, or so I thought. One day, she decided to climb the infamous picket fence at San Rafael school as we waited for my mother to pick us up. Anything she did, I would follow suit. This would become a trend, and later I followed her to college after I graduated from high school. My sister was always my protector and my best friend. I was always the annoying little sister. As she went up the fence, I followed. Both of us were at the top when my mom arrived and yelled for us to come. As I turned to look at my mother, my right arm was punctured by the picket. I looked back at the blood rushing down my arm, onto the fence, and the ground. Oddly enough, I never freaked out. Perhaps I had become numb to feelings as a result of the sexual fondling. The freaking out I left to my mother. The yelling of "Virgen de Guadalupe," which can be translated to "Oh God," was a common occurrence in our household. I was rushed to the hospital with my skin literally hanging off. The doctor said, "I am going to cut this skin off, since it can't be reattached. This may hurt some." The doctor cut the excess piece of skin that was hanging off my arm. I looked at that piece of skin sitting on a metallic tray. As I looked at it, it began to die and curl up at the ends. I related to that piece of skin, because deep down, I too was dying—of embarrassment. Again, I did not cry during this entire ordeal. This was the first instance of me not showing any emotion during what would have easily been a horrific or traumatic experience for anyone. To this day, this story is a fan favorite—and I have an interesting scar to show for it.

One Sunday morning, my sister and I scurried up the wrought iron staircase to my grandfather's door. When we received our regular Sunday chocolate bar, my sister turned around and bumped into me on accident. This caused me to fall backward and roll down the two-story flight of stairs. Before I even hit the bottom, my mother screamed, "Virgen de Guadalupe," her voice blaring through the courtyard walls. I finally hit the bottom, got up, and said, "I am fine." My mother, on the other hand, was not. She had fainted from my fall. Once again, I shed no tears. It was no big deal . . . all was good.

Soon we would be leaving this country, and this life, never to return again. My parents would eventually sell the little yellow house, and we would venture to the north to live the American dream. We did not know what to expect. I welcomed the change and was open to moving to a different country. I was excited, and I was ready.

CHAPTER 2

CHICAGO

In 1988, my mother put all three of us on a plane en route to Chicago. We waved goodbye to her before turning to walk down the long, narrow bridge onto the plane. My mother told Eddie, the oldest of us, "Take care of your sisters." A family member would be picking us up at the airport in Chicago. My father wanted to stay in Mexico, but my mother wanted more for us. She wanted us to grow up in the United States, to go to college, and to have a future. I imagined that my mother and father were staying behind while they made arrangements to come to the U.S., since at the time, they were not yet U.S. citizens. We were moving to the U.S., after all, and my siblings and I were U.S. citizens. Though we were citizens already, the U.S. was a whole new world—and Chicago was extremely cold. We were far away from our cozy yellow stucco home. Yet, only being six years old, it didn't occur to me to question the move. I was excited and open to change.

We moved into the basement apartment of a friend of a family member. It was nothing like what we were used to, but it was our new home. The Riveras were very nice and kind to us. The couple had three daughters, Martha, Carmen, and Karina, along with two sons, Javier and Manuel. We quickly got along with them and felt comfortable. I will never forget that the basement apartment, our new home, had an antique furnace with a small crack in the middle. This furnace scared me. It made odd crackling noises, and I always imagined the fire would somehow escape. I had never seen a furnace, nor did we ever need such a thing in Guadalajara with its beautiful weather.

Chicago is one of the most diverse—yet segregated—cities in the world. Different neighborhoods are separated by streets and bridges. Cicero, where we lived, is a low-income suburb of Chicago made up of predominantly Mexican immigrants. As if an unwritten rule, most Mexicans lived on the West side of Cicero Ave, while the African Americans lived on the East side. We stayed on our side, period. Cicero was by no means a safe neighborhood; there was crime and plenty of gang activity. No one would dare walk near Cermak and Cicero Ave at night. Cicero is mostly known for Al Capone, as well as the crime and corruption that came with his era. Capone's original home is still one of the most beautiful homes in the neighborhood.

One morning, we woke up to find bloody footprints starting from the front walkway of the home leading all the way to the back walkway. I looked down at the footprints and wondered what happened to the person who left them there. Carmen, Natalie, and I observed the footprints closely and realized that this person with bloody feet had been walking on their tiptoes. The footprints were odd, scary to us children, and unexplainable. The footprints stayed on the sidewalk until they were washed away by the rain. Despite the scary furnace and suspicious bloody footprints, life in this little apartment was fun. We played with Carmen, the youngest of the sisters, and her brother Javier. Carmen was a year older than my sister, and Javier was my brother's age. Carmen and Natalie would choreograph little dances and had a secret girl's club. Though I was not invited to be a part of their club, I somehow, someway, managed to always tag along for the fun and try to dance their dances. I was not going to be left behind.

It wasn't long before I made another trip to the ER. Trips to the ER were becoming quite familiar at this point. One Saturday afternoon, my sister and I had gotten our hands on some Pixy Stix candy. I watched as my sister put the unopened Pixy stick in her mouth and cut the other end open with scissors. She handed me the scissors and, of course, not being quite as precise with my cutting, I cut into the left side of my lip. The blood instantly gushed down my chin and onto the ground. My sister wore a mortified expression as I walked over to where my mother was. You can guess what happened—she invoked her infamous "Virgen de Guadalupe." My mother grabbed a towel and put it over my lip, which was practically hanging off my face. What is up with these freak accidents all my life? Again, I was indifferent about the entire ordeal—no tears, no big deal. At the ER, the doctor looked at me with his green eyes and said he could put me back together. I do not remember his name, but wherever he is, he did a splendid job. The left side of my lip had been hanging off, and I must have looked like a zombie from Michael Jackson's *Thriller* video. This doctor managed to stitch my severed lip with only the slightest evidence that anything had happened. In fact, my lips are one of my best physical assets today. But if you look closely, there is a small bump in the inside of my lip where it was sewn back on.

Soon it was time for me to enter kindergarten. On the first morning, my mother fixed my hair in pigtails and sent me off to Cicero School. I was excited and looking forward to my new school, and I was happy that I did not have to wear a hideous uniform. As I arrived in my classroom, I suddenly realized that I could not understand what the teacher or kids were saying. The kids did not look like me; they had white skin, mostly had light-colored eyes, and did not speak Spanish. They were speaking English. I knew some English words, but by no means did I understand what they were saying. The kids were making fun of me and calling me Pippi Longstocking. I had no idea who that was, and I had no idea why I was in this class. I was just going to have to learn English, and figure the rest out as I went along. I soon realized what it was to be a Mexican, brown-skinned, freckled-faced, Spanish-speaking little girl in the U.S. I was different from the other kids, and I was being made fun of for it.

That day after school I told my mother, "The kids were speaking English, and they were making fun of my pigtails. Can you not put my hair like this anymore?" It turns out I was supposed to be in a bilingual class, and was put in the wrong class by accident. Thank God that mistake was corrected the next day, and I was put in a class with kids who looked like me and spoke like me.

It would take three years for my parents to save enough money for us to buy a place of our own. We didn't move far, just a few blocks away. My parents purchased a two-flat red-brick building. We lived on the second floor of this two-flat for two years, and rented out the first floor.

My parents worked extremely hard and long. Both worked factory jobs. They were chasing the American dream, saving every penny, and making sure their children had everything they needed. We always had food, clothes, fun, and even vacations. But with their hardworking lifestyle came the fact that we were latchkey kids. In the mornings we did not have our parents; we only had each other. We dressed ourselves, fed ourselves, and walked to school by ourselves. We never had the luxury of having our parents wake us up for school. After school we would come home and make mayonnaise sandwiches, watch TV, and wait for mom to come home from work. We spent many hours alone, but we were good, independent children. Thank God we never found ourselves in trouble. This two-flat also had a large basement in which we would play Nintendo, play with our dolls, and watch TV. It is scary to believe that we were left home alone so often, which, these days, might warrant a call to Child Protective Services. But for us, it was the norm. My parents had to work to keep food on the table and a roof over our heads.

During the summers, with no school, we were left alone for even longer hours than usual. My sister and I would sneak out of the house to go swimming. This was obviously forbidden by our mother. But it was summer, we were hot, and too independent for our own good. My sister was nine and I was seven, and we would spend entire days at Parkholme Pool. And, like clockwork, my mother would pull up at 4 p.m. and scream at us to get in the car. We would run out of the pool, dripping water into her car. We would get a scolding, but it was well worth it. We had the best time.

Education had been drilled into our brains as being the most important thing to ever pursue. At an incredibly young age, my father sat all three of us down and said, "You have two options: go to school and become something, or go bust your back in the factory like your mother and me." He would raise his left hand and show us his three missing fingers. In the factory, he had got his hand stuck in a machine and lost portions of his thumb, pointer and middle fingers. We listened to his advice, and chose the route of education. In the winter, we walked to school in the bitter cold among the tall piles of snow. At least it was only about two miles and not ten, although it sometimes felt that long.

CHAPTER 3

THE NICE SIDE OF TOWN

My parents had always been frugal with their money. The summer before I entered fifth grade, they were able to move us into a gorgeous home where we would live for the next eight years. We were so excited when my parents took us to see our new house for the first time. It was a beautiful two-story white-brick house with stairs that curled up to the second floor. This home was a dream. Best of all, it was on the "nice" side of Cicero. It was also on the last block of Cicero, the furthest west. The further west you went, the nicer and more expensive the homes and neighborhoods became. It was a beautiful neighborhood with a wide street, and we even had Caucasian neighbors. At that time, we thought that if white people lived in a neighborhood that meant it was a nice neighborhood. My parents had worked extremely hard to be able to purchase this beautiful home.

A new home also meant a new school. I would be attending Lincoln School for fifth grade. Even more exciting, our aunt lived right across the street from our new home. Lincoln was a nice school, being the school in the "nice" side of Cicero. But because of the high incidence of gang activity in Cicero, all the kids from the rough side were bussed to the nice school. This meant that many gang members attended my school. One day while sitting in English class, gunshots were fired through the windows. This wasn't a daily occurrence, but we did occasionally spend time under our desks dodging bullets. We were all unfazed by the gun violence. After so long, the initial shock eventually wore off.

Lincoln is where I had my first kiss, met my first real boyfriend, and made some great friendships. It's also where I first met Joaquin, who attended Lincoln for a short time before he moved to a different school. I would later reconnect with him in high school, where he would become my angel on Earth. Lincoln is also where I first laid eyes on the boy who would later be my first real experience of young love. I made some great friends at Lincoln, and as a new student in fifth grade, I was welcomed and had no issues fitting in. The most interesting thing about Cicero was the large number of elementary schools on different sides of the neighborhood. When we were in grade school, the kids from the various schools were all rivals, but once we graduated eighth grade, we would all be going to the same high school together.

In fifth grade I was somewhat awkward and not comfortable in my own skin. I began to pay attention to my body and how it was developing. I felt insecure and was not too fond of the way I looked. Like any other young girl, I compared myself to other girls. I wasn't overweight, but just a little chubby. I thought that losing weight might heal this feeling of discomfort. One day, my sister and I were hanging out at home alone during a holiday. I felt a sharp pain on my left side. It was debilitating and I started to cry. Natalie became scared and didn't know what to do. My mother was at work and it would take an hour for her to arrive home. Natalie called our mom and told her that I was in a lot of pain and wanted to go to the hospital. Our mother advised us to call our Aunt Lety, who took me to the ER. At this point, the ER had become a familiar place. I was wheeled into an MRI machine so they could try to find out what was going on. Their theory was that my appendix might need to come out. They decided to keep me in observation and hooked me up to an IV bag. They told my mother that they would monitor my blood every hour, and I would not be able to eat in the meantime. That afternoon in the hospital turned into a five-day stay. The doctors kept me from eating or drinking anything in case my appendix needed to be removed. During those five days, I did not eat a single thing. As one would imagine, after five days of no food I lost a lot of weight. I was finally discharged with no answers and my appendix still inside me. The doctors were clueless and said I was free to go home.

Thinking back as an adult, I realize that we were lucky to have insurance through my mother's job. I cannot even imagine how much a five-day hospital stay would have cost. When I arrived home, I took a look at my body. I had lost weight and I liked the way I looked. Those five days gave me a body I could start to love, but in my mind, I did not realize how weak and malnourished I was. I wanted to stay at this lower weight, and to do that, I needed to cut my food intake. This would be difficult, since my mother cooked amazing food (and because I loved to eat). Eating had always been a collaborative activity we enjoyed as a family. But since I was so active growing up, not being able to sit still, weight had never been an issue before. As I started cutting my meals down, I started seeing progress. I started shrinking and I was happy about that. I continued cutting down my meals during the summer leading into sixth grade. Then I began to stop eating overall; I became obsessed with my thin body. I was already thin—very thin—but my eyes didn't see that. I was suffering from anorexia, and it was evident. My mother would pack my lunch for school, but during lunchtime, I would throw the sandwich out and eat only the tangerine. It didn't take long for a custodian to realize my lunchtime habit. My body was thin, fragile, and my ribs were beginning to show. The custodian brought it up to my teacher, who pulled me out of class and asked me what was going on. She said, "You are my star student. Is everything okay at home?" Everything was fine, I told her. I could not let my secret of starving myself get out. It would derail my goal of losing more weight.

Anorexia is a horrible emotional disorder characterized by the obsessive desire to lose weight by refusing to eat. You see yourself as distorted, so you are dissatisfied with what you see. The skinnier you get, the more content you become. What you see in the mirror is not a true reflection of reality. My mother quickly saw that I had a problem and took me to a doctor who weighed me and did a full physical. The scale read eighty-nine pounds. I was five feet tall and weighed a mere eighty-nine pounds. The doctor said, "If you do not put on weight, we will have to admit you to the hospital and feed you through a tube." I considered the consequences, but I was definitely in too deep to stop.

My birthday was nearing. I had gone to a local pet store and had seen a gorgeous gray and white cockatiel with rosy circular cheeks and a gorgeous crest that stood up high on its head. The owner of the store would take him out and show me how sweet he was. He was adorable, and I wanted him. I masterminded a plan as to how I would ask my mother to let me have him. She did not like animals. My dad once brought home a kitten, but my mother made him give it away. I also had a white pet mouse, Speedy, that was gifted to me by my cousin, but my mom gave Speedy away too. She was very orderly, and our home was always immaculately clean. There was no room for a dirty rodent.

I came home from the pet store and pleaded to my dad that I wanted the cockatiel. I said, "Dad, what do I have to do to get this bird?" He of course replied, "Talk to your mother." I knew I had to bring my A game to really convince her that this bird was going to save me. I told her I would care for it, clean it weekly, and be responsible for it. To my amazement, she agreed. I was so excited. I was ten years old, about to turn eleven. I ran with excitement to my father and said, "Let's go get my bird!" My father looked at me with a smile, and said, "There's one condition." I said, "Okay, what is it?" He said, "You have to start eating and gain back some weight." I agreed.

I named the cockatiel Tony, but we would just call him Birdie. Birdie saved my life. He cured my anorexia. I was so enamored with this bird. He was adorable and loved me so much. He would walk around and pick at everything I put in front of him. He also sang gorgeously, and even learned to say a few words. He would also make kissing noises from the kissing noises I would make to him. He learned to say, "*vente*," which means "come here" in Spanish. When I got older, I took Birdie to college with me. He rode in my car for sixteen hours, squawking his head off all the way to Houston, Texas, where I moved in 2008. I was eleven years old when I got Birdie, and he is still alive and with me today. He is twenty-seven years old at the time of writing this book. He is losing his feathers and has arthritis in his legs. He is an old bird, still sings, but does not like to be bothered. Cockatiels have a lifespan of twenty-five years, and Birdie is still going strong.

CHAPTER 4

MORTON EAST HIGH SCHOOL

I was very excited to start high school. It was new territory, and I was going to be in school with my sister for two years. Morton East was an interesting school, to say the least. This school was immense, and we would get lost trying to navigate it. The five minutes they gave us between classes was never enough time to get to a class on the fourth floor from the first. You would think we were Olympic-class sprinters racing for a medal as we tried to get to class on time. Morton East was a school with gang activity, drugs, sex, violence, undocumented students, and rampant teenage pregnancy. In fact, when I was in high school, Morton East had the highest pregnancy rates in the country. Teenage pregnancy was a daily occurrence. Sophomore year was when most pregnancies happened. For some reason, everyone was having sex, and many were becoming pregnant. Pregnant students even had some privileges at our school. When a girl was pregnant, she was set up with an elevator pass, which was something of a luxury in this gargantuan school. Because of the high demand, babies of students were provided with free full daycare at the school. The daycare also served as early childhood development classes for students. How convenient! It was a win-win. The name of the game was do not end up pregnant.

Morton East had everything your typical high school has, including many social cliques. When I went to high school, social media didn't exist, and it was still hell to get through. I can only imagine what kids these days have to deal with. I became popular very quickly, which was not a good thing. When you're popular all eyes are on you, and you can easily become a target for rumors. I fell into the cliques with the smart and athletic kids. I was an advanced placement student and played soccer. AP classes and soccer kept me out of trouble—drugs, alcohol, and everything in between. In my freshman year, I quickly made many friends and even won freshman homecoming court. All the girls who wanted to run for homecoming court, along with the Senior Homecoming Queen, would put their names on a ballot in hopes of winning this popularity contest.

It did not take long for me to start dating a football player named Oscar. It made sense. He was sweet—even if somewhat aggressive and possessive—but also cute, and super athletic. I lost my virginity to Oscar. It happened so quickly that, to be completely honest, it was not very eventful at all. I was fifteen years old, and never had a conversation with my parents about sex. This topic was not something commonly discussed in a Catholic Mexican household. When it came to sex, the answer was simple—you did not have it. That relationship fizzled out.

Sophomore year I fell in love, and this was the type of love your teenage heart skips a beat over. I always thought Emilio was incredibly attractive. He was a year older than me, played basketball, was dark, and had hazel eyes—he was simply adorable. I was completely smitten with him. Among friends, I had mentioned that I thought Emilio was adorable, and a week later his friend asked me what I thought about him. A week after that, he showed up at an after-school club event and asked me out. We fell in love, and it was amazing. He was my first love.

We had a lot of fun, but the fun was short-lived. In the summer of 1999, Emilio's sister was brutally murdered, decapitated, and dismembered. This crime was one of the most vicious crimes in the history of Chicago. Emilio's existence was crushed into pieces. In his pain, our relationship did not survive. I was not only torn from the breakup but also from what had happened to his sister. How does an adolescent wrap their mind around an event like that? Losing Emilio was the most pain I had ever felt as a sixteen-year-old. But losing him on top of this disaster destroyed me. It was a lot to comprehend. Being this young, in love, and in the midst of tragedy was a recipe for disaster.

I wanted to be there for him, but he had moved on. My mind was lost, and I soon fell into the deepest depression imaginable. I could not function; my sadness overpowered me. I could not bear going to his sister's funeral. My depression got so bad, I started missing school. I spent days in bed and hours staring into the abyss of sadness, completely dazed. I could not sleep. I could not eat. I am sure Emilio went through the same emotions. He did often reach out to me to make sure I was okay, to which I would nod and go about my day. Despite our relationship ending, we were forever connected as a result of this traumatic situation. Years later we reconnected in 2005 after I graduated college. We got together and spent time with each other. It was nice to see each other again and reminisce about our adolescence. We even tried dating again, but we were in different places in our lives; our lives just did not align anymore. Ultimately, this experience of despair and tragedy was the reason I went to work for the government. I wanted to know how people could commit such heinous acts.

While I was dealing with my own breakup and tragedy, my best friend Lucia had become pregnant and was going through the shock of it. Lucia was like a sister to me, and the two of us were inseparable. We met through mutual friends, and she was the most adorable Filipina girl I had ever seen. We shared so much, even the same last name, and we promised each other our daughters would be named the same. She was having a girl, and had already picked out the name for her daughter. Soon after, Lucia's mother moved her away from Morton East, and just like that she was gone. When she left, my heart ached. Lucia also fell into a deep depression, having to deal with both moving away and caring for a child at such a young age. We would talk every day after school. Our depression was so powerful, we even had a pact that if we decided to kill ourselves, we would do it together. The plan was that we would sit in a car inside the garage and simply die together. Lucia was admitted into an inpatient care facility, and it did not take long for me to follow.

My AP Spanish teacher, Mrs. Roethke, pulled me out of class one day, rushed me to my counselor Gail's office. "Angelica cannot be in school. She needs treatment," they told my mother on the phone. I left school for an entire month and was admitted to outpatient treatment. I credit my recovery to Mrs. Roethke and my academic advisor, Gail. They showed me so much love and helped me through the hardest time of my adolescent life. If I ever felt like disconnecting from the world, Gail would allow me to sit in her office. She had an open-door policy for me, and I frequently took her up on the offer. I would hang out with Gail and talk about how amazing college would be. I was diagnosed with major depression and put on anti-depressant medication.

My dear friends, Joaquin and Beatriz, were there by my side through all of my pain. Both picked up the broken pieces and supported me unconditionally. They held my hand and promised it would all be okay. The love and support I received from these individuals brought me back to life. Even when I was receiving treatment, rumors still swarmed wildly. Apparently, according to the rumors, Joaquin had gotten me pregnant and I had left school as a result. Thinking back, we had a rough time in high school, each of us dealing with our own issues. But we sought solace in each other. These friendships were by far the strongest and most amazing I had ever experienced. Having someone there to love me and walk me through such a dark stage of my adolescent life was vitally important. Until this day Joaquin and I reminisce about our high school life and how hard it was to navigate. I am forever grateful to the friends who were there for me.

The adolescents at the outpatient treatment center I attended were brilliant. These kids questioned life deeply—and drove themselves crazy over it. I fit right in. We would have group therapy, class time, and play time. Most of the kids had their own traumatic experiences to share, and the mental health professionals were a godsend to us. I learned to appreciate them, love them, and be grateful to them. These adults were giving their time to youths who were lost in the despair of their own minds. Many of us recovered, and many came and went. I heard many stories of kids leaving only to find themselves back again soon after. The most disturbing of the kids were those who were convinced that as soon as they were let out, they were going to take their lives. What I learned is that when you decide to take your own life, the decision ultimately stems from the belief that being dead is a better option than being alive. In truth, many of these brilliant kids indeed took their own lives after being discharged. Suicide is an issue that is prevalent in adolescence, and sadly, far too many adolescents end their lives. I considered it myself. I discussed it and even had a plan in place. The difference is that I was heard and I survived to tell the story.

I continued going to weekly therapy sessions after completing my month-long outpatient treatment. My psychiatrist, Dr. Pai, was very dry and boring. He asked only how the medicines were working, and not much else. But I loved my therapist, Ms. Larson, and looked forward to my sessions with her. She was very confident and exuded so much sass. She always wore elegant silk scarves that were wrapped in various ways. In her therapy room, I voiced that I had been sexually molested as a child. It was the first time I had felt comfortable sharing that story with anyone. Together, we worked through so much, and I learned a great deal about myself. When our sessions ended, I was saddened that I would not talk to her again. She told me she had enjoyed our time together and that I should reach out for support while in college. I am eternally grateful to her and her calming, loving demeanor. Therapy is soul loving; it allows you to look deep inside yourself, deal with the demons, and then release them.

Luckily, I recovered and rebounded from my heartbreak. Lucia took me out to a hip-hop set in the North Side of Chicago. Hip-hop had been healing our hearts. While there, I met a handsome Colombian guy named Martin. He approached me with his big eyes and irresistible smile. He was different. He attended an all-boys private school and was highly intelligent and experienced. He was exciting, fun, and entertaining—he was exactly what I needed to get out of the dark place I had been in. Lucia, however, was not a fan of Martin. In fact, she hated him. Although Lucia would lie to my mom and tell her I was spending the night at her house so that I could be with him, she did not think he was good for me. She also felt like he was getting in between the close friendship that she and

I had. She felt that I was not being a good friend to her and that I was too caught up with Martin. Later, I missed the birth of her daughter, and she blamed it on Martin. One day she came to my house upset, voicing that I was a "shitty friend." My mother came down the stairs and asked her to leave.

Over the last twenty years, I tried reaching out to her on four separate occasions, but each attempt failed. However, on the fourth attempt, we reconnected. She came to meet me in my hotel room on the twelfth floor of the Viceroy in Chicago. She was still as adorable and fashionable as ever. Over a bottle of Clase Azul Tequila, we mended our friendship, updated each other on the last twenty years and laughed out loud. We spoke of our turbulent adolescence and vowed to rekindle our friendship. Seeing Lucia, hugging her, and listening to her share with me the last twenty years of her life filled my heart and soul with joy. We are friends again and are looking forward to many years in each other's lives. Making amends with our troubled past allowed for a new future to be born for us.

The relationship with Martin was short-lived. We had fun while it lasted. I was beginning to explore my sexuality for the first time. We were young and experimenting. He had his insecurities as much as I had mine. We ended up going to the same university and later found out he had gone to school with a girl who would become one of my best friends in college; it's a small world. We had many mutual friends in college and hung out from time to time. In high school, Martin always spoke about becoming an attorney. Today he is a partner at a reputable Chicago firm.

One day my mother was going through my personal items and found my birth control pills. I was seventeen years old, and had made the mature decision to protect of myself. I did not want to end up pregnant. I went to my family doctor, Dr. Velez, and told her that I wanted to be careful. She supported my decision. I told her that if my mother ever found out, to lie to her and tell her it was to regulate my period. Sure enough, my mother was mortified at her discovery. The mere idea that I was sexually active tore her apart. She grabbed me, and off we went to see Dr. Velez. My mother was so upset, she yelled at the doctor, "How dare you give this to my daughter without my consent!" The doctor looked at me and then told my mother, "Your daughter can make her own decisions about birth control." Then, as we had planned, she told my mother that she had put me on the pill to regulate my period. I exhaled a sigh of relief. She kept her word, and I came out of that situation unscathed. Fortunately, I no longer had to hide it. I was being careful and responsible.

The relationship between my mother and I was always a difficult one. Her beliefs and ideals did not align with mine at all. I was the black sheep of the family, always questioning everything— "why, why, why?" All I ever got was, "Because I said so." Not surprisingly, I ended up in a career where all I do is ask questions. I was extremely defiant and would often question my mother's authority. I did not like that my brother could have girls in his room, stay out late, and not have to check in, while my sister and I were prohibited from doing those same things. It angered me and made me rebellious. I would come home late, and my mother would be sitting on the couch, like a scary shadow in the dark. She would scare the crap out of me and say, "*Esta casa no es un hotel. ¿En dónde estabas?*" In English this means, "This house is not a hotel. Where were you?" Whenever I had a boyfriend, she was stricter with me; when I didn't, she let me be. I talked back to her a lot, which earned me a slap in the face on occasion. My father never hit me, but my mother would slap or hit me with the *chancla* (slipper). Once I came home late, and she chased me around the dining room table. I was far too fast for her to catch me, so she climbed on top of the table and raised her *chancla* to hit me. She ended up shattering the glass from the china cabinet behind her. The glass shattered on the ground like a million diamonds. She screamed, "Look what you made me do!" I just looked at her and laughed. The china cabinet remained unfixed for as long as I could remember.

Throughout high school, I built a strong circle of friends. It was composed of Joaquin, Beatriz, Jose, Roberto, and Juan. We were a fun and tight bunch. We would all pack into Jose's van to go stuff our faces at the local Chinese restaurant, go to the drive-in, or just hang out. At the drive-in, we would hide everyone in the back of the van and only pay for two tickets. Jimmy, Jose's little brother, would sneak in the van so he could come along too. This would anger Jose, but Jimmy was so cute and just wanted to hang with our group. We would climb out and sit on top of the van to enjoy the movie.

One night during my junior year of high school, we were out late studying for advanced placement exams. We were crammed into Roberto's new black two-door Toyota Celica en route to my house. I lived on the other side of town, which was a bit of a drive. The Cicero police must have seen Roberto's new car with temporary plates, because the next thing we knew we were all being put in the back of a paddy wagon and arrested for breaking curfew. Everyone was freaked out. I was mad and ready to talk some shit. We were taken to the Cicero Police Station, and all of us were put into a cell. I was very upset and decided to voice my opinion. I yelled at the cops that they were idiots, and that they had just locked up the smartest kids in the school. I remember saying to the cops that their children were going to be the lunch staff for ours. This was cringeworthy for sure. Joaquin kept telling me to shut up, and that I was making it worse for everyone. But I had conviction and was known to rip assholes for fun. All of our parents had to come to the station to pick us up. One by one they showed up, tired and pissed off—some were even drunk. I was the last to get picked up. I was never one to back down to authority, including law enforcement. I questioned everything, and that has not changed one bit. I later realized how terrifying this incident may have been to the others, but we can all laugh about it today.

The truth is, this wasn't the first time I had been arrested. During the summer of my sophomore year of high school in 1999, I was working as a lifeguard at Cermak Pool. At the time, I had a driving permit which allowed me to drive from home to work and back. My license was arriving any day. I was one block away from home when a rookie Cicero cop was stopped in front of me at a stop sign. The cop changed gears and instead of going forward, he drove backward into me. "Ugh, what an idiot!" I thought. He asked for my license and registration. I gave him my permit and, because he was a rookie, decided to arrest me. I told him, "You idiot, you crashed into me like an imbecile." The permit was legitimate, but he didn't know what else to do except arrest me. I told him, "I live a block away. Can we please stop at my parents' house and tell them what happened?" We stopped at my house, leaving my car parked a block away. I was sitting in the back of his cop car, how embarrassing. The cop got out and told my parents he had to take me in. My dad followed behind. I was taken to the Cicero Police Department, which was all the way on the other side of town. I was always really good at talking shit and stirring the pot. I asked him, "How did you even pass the academy?"

We arrived at the station, and as he sat me down on a bench, the cops there asked him, "What she do?" I yelled, "What did I do? Ask him what he did. He backed into my car at a stop sign, like an idiot!" The cops laughed; I am sure he was the rookie laughingstock of the office for at least a couple of weeks. A report was made, and I was released to my dad. It turns out the car was not damaged, but I was arrested for driving without a valid license. My license arrived three days after this stupid incident. The case was thrown out, and I was never fined or charged. But the arrest report remained on my record. I always thought a couple of arrests would make me look imperfect, but human, to the government. Years later, these incidents were discussed during my first top secret background investigation. The agents laughed about them. Ultimately, I was right—they added character.

My brother, my sister, and I always had a car because my parents were great at money management. They weren't brand new cars, but they were always practical. My sister and I shared a 1990 silver Nissan Sentra. When my sister left for college the car became mine, and I ended up totaling it in an accident. I ran a yellow light and crashed into a turning car. My friend Beatriz was in the car with me. Luckily, we did not get hurt, but the car was totaled. After that crash, my dad bought me a lovely baby blue 1992 Nissan Stanza. It was a gorgeous car. I used to pack about six of my soccer teammates in it and take them to practice after school. I had a lot of friends, but being popular also meant having a lot of haters. Some jealous, ghetto-ass girls broke the windshield and the front side windows twice. They know who they are. Besides the damage, what crushed me the most was that my dad was the one who had to pay to get the windows fixed. I was so ready to leave this ghetto-ass school, and all its drama.

All three of us Robles kids were extremely athletic and hardworking, which I definitely believe contributed to us being kept out of major trouble. We squeezed in school, work, and sports at the same time. We all had great work ethic, and loved making money. I even convinced my dad to sign a waiver when I was only fifteen years old so that I could work before the legal age of sixteen. At only fifteen, I worked at a clothing store at Riverside Park Mall, and later worked as a lifeguard at three different YMCA pools. I also worked at Cermak Pool in Lyons (a suburb of Chicago) for five summers. My sister also worked as a lifeguard. My brother worked at a theater and later as a pizza delivery guy for many years.

I ran track, played one year of volleyball, and three years of soccer. My sister played volleyball and was the pitcher on the girls' softball team. My brother played tennis and basketball. He was a great tennis player and won the high school state championship one year. He even earned a full scholarship to play tennis at Elmhurst College.

My sister and I liked being able to buy our own expensive brand-name clothes. At the time, the rich kids were wearing Abercrombie & Fitch. We weren't rich, but we worked. There was no way my parents were going to buy us sixty dollar jeans and forty dollar T-shirts. My brother has always been very frugal and didn't care for brand-name clothes. But he did like expensive tennis and basketball gear. Eddie has always been a huge saver. To this day, he calls his saving method "Eddienomics." Even after my parents sold the house, the new owner allowed Eddie to stay in his original room and pay minimal rent. Eddie joked that he came with the house. Since my brother's room was in the basement, he had his own living area and bathroom. The new owner traveled frequently, so my brother became the home's real caretaker. Eddie finally moved out of that basement in 2008 when I left for Houston. He moved into my condo with all of my furniture and other things that I left behind. He requested that I provide him with an itemized list of every single item in the condo, down to the last fork. The only things I took with me were my boyfriend, my birdie, my clothes, and my car.

In my senior year of high school, I already had one foot out the door. I couldn't wait to get the hell out of that school and move on. In fact, I had earned so many advanced placement (AP) credits that I was already a sophomore in college. I disconnected from high school clubs and most people, but maintained my participation on the soccer team. I was ready to leave and never look back. I applied to many schools and was accepted into all of them—including Ivy-League schools. I was in the top 10% of my class and had a high grade point average (GPA) from taking so many AP classes. I also earned the Coca-Cola Scholarship. Coming out of my deep depression, my parents wanted me to stay close in case I might need an intervention. Looking back now, I wish I would have had the courage to go to an Ivy League school, but the trajectory of my life would have changed completely.

It did not take long for me to enter my next relationship. In my senior year of high school, I ended up in my first toxic relationship. Luís was a singer in an alternative-music band who was obsessed with The Smashing Pumpkins. We were polar opposites, the oddest coupling ever, but for some strange reason, our relationship continued for longer than it should have. I think we ended up together partly because my friend Beatriz was dating Luís' best friend, Adrian. The relationship became extremely sexual. We had a lot of sex, and it was addictive. I believe the sex between us was the only thing keeping our relationship alive. For two years, I believed we were in love. We did not have much in common other than the physical enjoyment each other provided.

CHAPTER 5

WTF!?

I sat in my grandfather's car, looking at a porn video through a camcorder that he had handed me. This was weird, awkward, and wrong on so many levels. I turned eighteen in the November of my senior year, and I began to realize that my mother would sometimes complain about me to my grandfather, her father, Ricardo. My mother had a close relationship with her father, and he was the patriarch of the family. Although he had his great qualities, he was also a nasty man. My grandfather waited until I turned eighteen, and then started to talk to me about sex. I thought this was super weird, and to myself, I thought, "This ship has sailed." He spoke about how he was so strict with his daughters, and how they got married incredibly young as virgins, and most of their marriages had failed. He blamed himself for their divorces. He said to me, "You have to explore, have sex, and learn how to please a man." My first thoughts were, "What the fuck?" So he showed me porn videos and told me, "This is how it's done." After the initial shock of what happened wore off, I tried to ignore it and think of him as just an old pervert.

He told me that he was still having sex even at his old age, and that in fact, he was paying girls from my school $500 to sleep with him. I believed him, because at this point, it was evident that he was a nasty fuck. The sum of $500 was a lot of money for any poor girl at Morton East. He told me how he would bring the girls to my aunt's house across the street and have sex with them. He also said he would teach me how to please a man, but I had to keep it a secret and not tell anyone.

At the time, I was working with my aunt at her communication company. My grandmother would make lunch for me every day, and my grandfather would bring it to me. One day, he walked towards me, pinned me to the wall, and attempted to put his hands down my shirt. I pushed his frail six-foot body away from me. I told him that he was crazy and that I would say something. I went home and immediately told my sister, who was of course horrified. She said he had never spoken to her about anything like that. I figured he must have thought of me as easy bait to fuel his nasty, incestuous fantasies. My sister was boiling with anger. She called him and ripped him a new asshole. She told him, "You are dead to us." For the next fourteen years, we would act as if everything was okay and go about our lives as if nothing had happened. We eventually told my mother, but she, along with all of our aunts for that matter, had been brainwashed by him.

Other instances came to light where he had shown some of my girl cousins the same porn videos he had shown me—he even got caught doing it! But in my mother's family, this kind of shit would happen, and it would be swept under the rug. It was never discussed. Soon, that rug was full of nasty lumps. I do believe his own daughters were aware of how much of a pervert their father really was, but they tried to convince themselves it wasn't true. After his death, I reached out to some of my girl cousins, and they confessed that he had also told them to explore their sexuality. Years later I brought it up to my mother again, and she was completely mortified. She was convinced I had never told her. This was an indication of how much of a mental hold he had on his family, and my mother in particular.

My relationship with my mother has come a long way. As an adult, I was able to heal a lot of the damaged emotions of my youth. We are close, and love each other very much. I understand that she was trying to keep me safe and out of trouble. And I understood that I was extremely defiant. But it is that defiance that builds successful CEOs, business owners, and the shakers and movers of the world. I learned to love her for who she is. I learned to listen to her and not talk back. I better understand many of her decisions now that I have a five-year-old daughter myself; a daughter who is, in many ways, 100% more defiant than I ever was. I am ready for the challenge.

Before my grandfather died, I had two conversations with him. The first was at his home in San Antonio. I told him that I forgave him because I had let go of the pain and shame of what he had done to me. He brushed the conversation off as any true avoidant would do. He just said everything was fine and that nothing happened. Which is exactly what I had heard growing up. Things would happen—uncles would get drunk, fight, drive off angry after a fight, sometimes even drive off drunk on the wrong side of the street—and the next week, everything was fine. The second time I tried having this conversation was on what we thought would be his death bed. My grandfather had been sick in the hospital and had one of his cancerous lungs removed. I went to visit him, held his hand, and had a moment alone with him. I told him again that I forgave him, and I no longer held him accountable for my shame. He just looked at me and nodded. I was free from all that shame, guilt, and embarrassment.

Families come with deep, dark secrets. I am unveiling some in this book, but many others remain. When people are used to their particular family dynamic or norm, the cycle tends to repeat itself. Nothing is a shock anymore, and the new normal is actually pretty frightening. One of my uncles is engaged to his first cousin—that is, his mother's sister's daughter. They are totally open on social media about it, and they claim to love each other. Other members of the family "love" the photos they post online. In my opinion, this is wrong on so many levels, but the mentality is that "love does not have boundaries." That is exactly the problem: there are no boundaries, and there were never any boundaries. One can wonder how their family of origin did a number on their own mental well-being and decision making. At this point, nothing surprises me. I have seen it all, heard it all, and experienced more than any "ordinary" human would or should experience. But I am not ordinary. My experiences have made me extraordinary.

CHAPTER 6

CONNECTING WITH THE AFTERLIFE

My grandfather ended up living for years after having his lung removed. When he finally passed, everyone flew to Florida to be by his side. He died surrounded by most of his kids, his wife, and a lot of his grandchildren. I knew the moment he passed, because I have always had an incredibly special intuition when it comes to the spirit world. As a child, I had seen and heard ghosts in Mexico, in the U.S., and still to this day. I was sitting on my couch at home, and I saw and felt a massive gush of wind barrel down my staircase and shoot past me. That was my grandfather's sign that he was now free. One minute later my mother called me in tears and told me he had passed. I simply told her, "I know."

His wife, my grandmother Guadalupe, or Bela, as we called her, died a few years later. I got to see her before she died, and she got to meet my daughter, Belén. My grandmother and I had a very special connection. When I would experience paranormal activity, she was the only one who believed me. No one else, not even my mother, would validate my feelings and experiences. My grandmother, on the other hand, told me that I was special and that she believed me. When someone close to me died, they would come to visit me either in movement, shadows, whispers, dreams, or energy. I have never shared this with anyone until now, but when my Uncle Reynaldo died when I was in sixth grade, I heard him whispering to me in my room. He was saying that everything was going to be okay. I wrote a poem about my uncle and later raised money in his honor. I didn't deal very well with the concept of death, and became extremely afraid of it.

When my grandmother died, she too came to visit my mother and I. My mother suffered a lot when her mother died. Bela appeared to my mother, sitting on her bed, holding her hand, caressing it, and telling her that she was now in a good place. When I was pregnant with my second child, I went to live with my mother while our house was being built. I would often feel my grandmother caressing my back like she used to do when I was scared, frightened, or sad. I knew it was her. I could feel her presence. My daughter Belén was a baby at the time, and she would wake at night and lift her arms up from her crib as if someone was there to pick her up. We saw her doing this many nights through the baby cam. Later, my daughter would tell us that a lady with curly hair had visited her, which I am sure was my grandmother. My daughter would also mention that she had a sister in heaven, which was the baby I miscarried before I had my son, Zion.

The paranormal has always been a big part of my life. Every time I go to a new place, I always sense the energy of that place. When I was moving to Houston as an adult, I viewed a home that was being sold at an extreme discount. We walked through the home, and I told my parents that something had happened in that house. I felt a dark sadness in my chest. When I researched the home later, I discovered the husband had shot the wife and then killed himself there. Another instance happened when my husband and I went to Flatonia, Texas, where his aunt had rented a beautifully restored old home. I did not sleep that night. I felt bad energy and spirits.

When we ventured to the basement, we noticed strange hooks on the basement ceiling, as if sacrifices had been conducted in the home. My husband, Ray, would never validate me and thought I was just being paranoid.

I worked with a company called Equilibria, and my boss and colleagues, Rosalinda, Lewis, Ben, and Ian all stayed at the Menger Hotel, where we were doing a sports conference. The Menger Hotel is situated next to the Alamo, in San Antonio. This hotel is known to be haunted. I could feel a lot of energy when we arrived. In fact, I could feel something or someone touching my shoulder as we walked through the hotel. That night, Rosalinda went to bed listening to music, but I did not sleep. I was up all night just staring around the room. A plastic bag we had brought began to float around the room. Rosalinda was not buying it. I watched as the bag floated about the room. Later, Lewis told us that he had been recording a video with his cameraman, Michael, and Ian. They could hear voices and whispers when they played back the audio.

Even as a child living in Mexico, my sister and I saw an apparition on one of my uncle's ranches. A woman who looked white wearing a long dress was moving about the property. Everyone said she was "*La Llorona*," a woman who had drowned her children. I do not remember this instance as clearly as my sister, but as a child in our home in Mexico, I would often see apparitions of children and a woman. I was scared and frightened. I would always pray, and they would go away. Unfortunately, some apparitions were not as calm. When I was a teenager, I would see a shadow walk around my room, and it would pull my hair, mess with my sheets and change the station on my radio. During my adolescence, I used to sleep listening to jazz music because it brought me comfort. In my condo when I was living in Cicero, I would hear the floor creaking as if someone were walking. In that condo, there was always a sense that someone was watching you. Even when I moved out and my brother moved in, his girlfriend at the time also said her hair was sometimes pulled by a spirit.

The most recent instance of the paranormal was last year. I went to Santa Barbara to work at the Federal Penitentiary in Lompoc, California. I took my husband along, since it was gorgeous wine country. I was interrogating while he was enjoying the wine. We stayed on a gorgeous property that had a historical home and small cottages. The owner of the property offered us a tour of the home. In the living room, my attention immediately became focused on an old chair. I told the owner that I feel spiritual energy in the room, and I pointed at the seat. He said, "That is interesting, my mother died on that chair." I have always known that I have a special connection with the afterlife.

The afterlife is a touchy subject for many. I do believe that our past loved ones are always around. I can sense, hear, and feel them. I mostly feel my grandmother. But when I do go to places where spirits are around, I can feel them. I believe the spirits utilize energy from lights or other objects to communicate with us. Since my grandmother passed, I keep a picture of her in my room, and I see the lights flicker on occasion. Usually this happens when I have a big decision to make, almost as though she is there telling me to go with my gut instinct.

CHAPTER 7

UNIVERSITY OF ILLINOIS

My sister had been studying at the University of Illinois at Urbana-Champaign. U of I seemed like a safe route, since the school was far enough away from home, but still close enough that if shit hit the fan again, I could easily come home. I was going away to school, and my boyfriend Luís was unsure of his future and our relationship. We were going to try and make it work. The two-and-a-half-hour drive, long-distance relationship would not last long. It also didn't take long for him to stray, since I was away at college.

I opted to room with a random person in hopes of making a great friend. Allison, my new roommate, was a tall, skinny, blonde-haired, blue-eyed girl from the rich Chicago suburbs. She wasn't one bit excited that I was her roommate. We were quite different. She became obsessed with joining one of the popular sororities. U of I had one of the largest Greek systems in the country. She spent her nights drinking and trying to impress other girls so that she could be invited to their rich white sororities. One night she came home so drunk that she pulled her pants down and peed on the floor. I was so mortified that I went to sleep next door in the dorm of my friends Sophie and Missy.

Allison did not like my boyfriend. He would visit almost every other weekend, and all we would do is have sex, eat, and repeat. I soon gained a reputation for having loud sex. Surprisingly, I never got in trouble, formally. My boyfriend came to visit so often that I failed all my first semester classes. It was a sex-driven and toxic relationship. We would fight like cats and dogs, and then make up. The distance was taking a toll on his sex drive, and we were growing apart. During breaks from school, we would fight and break up just to get back together again. It was a sick back-and-forth dance. At some point, he no longer wanted to be in the relationship, but I tried to hold on to him as long as I could. His infidelity hurt me, but when it happened, he was honest about it. The relationship ended. I was crushed, but also relieved that it was over.

My three new friends from the dorm—Sophie, Missy, and Ana— were always there to pick up the pieces. In fact, they would hear me cry uncontrollably, and all three of them would come waltzing in. They were so much fun! Sophie and Missy roomed together next door, and Ana was in the room next to them. The four of us got very close and had a great time in college. I grew especially close with Sophie, a fun-loving Ecuadorian-Colombian girl. She came from an all-girls private school on the North side. Sophie was (and still is) smart, stylish, loyal, reliable, caring, hilarious, moody, and full of life. She was not afraid to speak her mind. She has always been very realistic and logical. She walked into my dorm the morning after Allison peed on the floor like a little puppy and told her, "Allison, I heard you had a rough night." When I failed my first semester, Sophie said, "No worries, we will make a report card to give to your mom." This was 2001, and paper report cards were still being issued. Sophie sat in front of her computer and created an entire fraudulent report card, complete with the U of

I emblem. It looked amazingly real. She was also very realistic in the grades she gave me. We printed it out, and I handed it to my mother who glanced at it, and said, "Okay, great!" My mother never even questioned why I was home a whole month early. Later, at my wedding, we told my mom about the fraudulent report card. Sophie has become one of my best friends and has been through it all with me.

I gravitated towards Sophie because there were not many minorities that attended U of I, and we stuck out. It made sense that Martin and I had mutual friends there—because so few Hispanics attended U of I. Even in college, racial groups self-segregated. We Hispanics and Blacks stuck together. College was the first time I met a person from India. No Indians lived in Cicero. The Hispanics and Blacks had few sororities and fraternities. Most of the big, lavish sorority and fraternity homes belonged to predominantly white, rich sororities and fraternities.

During my sophomore year, my parents decided to sell our beautiful two-story white-brick home and move to Houston, Texas. My parents were tired of the cold, the snow, and the grind. So home was now in a suburb of Houston called Sugar Land. They also bought two two-bedroom condos in Urbana, Illinois. My sister and I would live in one (we shared the condo *and* a computer), and the other was rented out. My sister Natalie was part of an intensive five-year engineering program and would come and go at all times of the day. I was extremely obsessive-compulsive and wanted everything to be a certain way. My sister was very busy, and as a result, was very messy too. Her room constantly looked like a tornado had passed through it. I had crazy rules: I didn't want toothpaste on the bathroom mirror, water puddles outside of the bathtub, or lights on past my bedtime. I used to yell at my sister when the light shone under the bottom sliver of my door. I was a psychology and chemistry major with a minor in OCD.

My sister did not like Luís one bit. She thought he was a waste of time and a loser. When my relationship ended, I grabbed our picture and threw it against the wall, the glass shattering into pieces. After my relationship ended, I vowed to myself that I was going to work, save as much money as possible, not date, abstain from sex, have fun on occasion, but mostly focus. I wanted to land internships and important experience in order to fill my resume with greatness. I picked up many odd jobs: I worked at Smoothie King, I worked as a traffic and pedestrian counter, and I even interned at the local domestic violence and homicide unit. I got to see all types of crazy shit there, including a cut-off ear in a jar and pictures from murder scenes. I wanted to become exposed to these types of things early so that when I did go to work for the government as an investigator, like I'd planned, it wouldn't be a big deal. I had the opportunity to read through violent reports. One cop said, "By the time you are done here, you will be able to eat lunch after seeing a crime scene."

The most exciting job I had by far was as an on-call youth crisis worker. This job paid great money, but it came with a price. I had to be on call several nights a week and carry a pager. The nights I was on call, the pager would beep, and I had to head out. The job entailed picking up delinquent youths from jail following a fight with their parents, running away, or an arrest. At the time, I was only nineteen. The kids ranged in age from ten to sixteen. University of Illinois is a campus literally in the middle of the Illinois cornfields. I cannot begin to count how many kids jumped out of my car and ran into the dark mazes of corn. I would scream out to them, "I'm not following you, bye." My job was to secure a temporary living arrangement for the kids. Usually that arrangement was either a family member, friend, group home, or juvenile detention center. I would go through a mental health assessment and ask these kids personal questions. They were receptive and would answer honestly. They all had their own stories of abuse, molestation, rape, addiction, depression, and suicidal thoughts. I saw myself in these kids and enjoyed the job. I learned to earn their trust and be a calming presence for them in their moments of despair.

Being on call during nights meant that my friends always had a designated driver. Obviously, I could not consume alcohol due to the nature of the job, since I could get paged at any random time. Sometimes I would be out with my friends, and if the pager went off, they knew they would need to find another ride home. I got called often; the youth of the cornfields were fucked up. I would watch as my friends got drunk and had a good time. I did not mind not being able to drink, myself. Alcohol was one of the things I wouldn't often engage with anyway. But when I did drink, I liked to party, get drunk, and dance my ass off. When I wasn't on call, I would definitely let loose. The only downside was the sleepless nights from dealing with at-risk youth and their crazy antics. But the job also came with some perks. My boss would write letters to my professors explaining my duties, and I would get out of tests. Sometimes these letters gave me extra days to study for exams.

I was not interested in making any new friends, since the ones I had made were enough for me. Sophie had introduced me to some of her friends—Leslie from back home, and Jennifer. Jen was a year older and had gone to high school with Sophie. Jen, Sophie, and I would become close and have the time of our lives. I would go to class, keep to myself, study, go to work, and do my workouts. I was saving lots of money and taking about eighteen hours worth of classes each semester. I was on a path to eventually work for the government. I realized that I had a lot of unresolved and pent-up anger. When I would get mad, lamps or other objects went flying. I hoped this anger would translate to me being a badass interrogator.

During my last year of college I was taking a leisure studies class. I would go to class, do my work and pay no mind to anyone in those huge auditorium classes with hundreds of students. One day, the leisure studies professor announced that we would be doing a group project. Ugh . . . I hated group projects because that meant that I would be doing most of the work. I dreaded this so much. A guy who was sitting a couple of seats away from me said, "Hey, you want to be partners?" As I heard his voice, I turned to look at him. My eyes widened; he was so damn attractive. *My God,* I thought to myself, *have you been sitting here this whole freaking semester?* Ben was a Brad Pitt look-alike. He never believed it, but he was. He had piercing blue eyes, almost transparent, and a warm, inviting smile. After I got over the shock of his ridiculously good looks, I said, "Sure." The professor announced that we needed to have at least three people in our group, so we roped in an Indian student who was sitting nearby.

Ben was so good for me. He was religious, a virgin, and so much fun. He liked to cook, tell corny jokes, eat hamburgers, and make out heavily. We started hanging out due to the project but soon became boyfriend and girlfriend. It happened very fast. I had vowed to not be romantically involved with anyone, because I had a mission, and because I had been so hurt from my last relationship. I kept our relationship on the low from my friends. In fact, he never met Sophie, Missy, Ana, or Jen. We spent our nights eating, talking, cuddling, and having the best long make-out sessions. He had a fun roommate who would do hilarious impersonations of

Bill Cosby. Ben was a junior, and I was in my last semester of college. I was graduating early, having completed three years of college, including failing my first semester. College had been easy for me. Having missed so many classes, most of my learning was self-taught—I only showed up during exams.

My new hot boyfriend was very sweet and caring. He was a nice distraction. My sister knew about him. In fact, one day Ben cooked food for her and her boyfriend at his apartment. I was still very standoffish with him and never invited him to my apartment. I kept him at arm's length, and since there was no sex involved, I could not become too enmeshed with him. Sex changes everything in a relationship. We basically avoided the question of what we would do once I graduated college. We talked about us visiting each other, but I knew he was not too excited about coming to Chicago to visit. In my heart, I knew this relationship would be over. He was originally from St. Louis, and Chicago was far away. I was getting ready to graduate.

In November of 2004, one month before I graduated college, I decided to get a Pap smear. I would be graduating soon, and would not have health benefits for a while. I had been to the doctor a mere three months prior. To my despair, my doctor called me and told me I had precancerous and cancerous cells on my cervix. In shock, I said, "Okay, so what do we do?" She said she would conduct a LEEP procedure, which meant burning off the cancer cells. I immediately made the appointment, and the procedure was done in the office. As I spread my legs, the doctor said it was going to be uncomfortable. Uncomfortable was not the right word to describe this; it was excruciating. I had half of my cervix burned off. I could smell the burning as she did it. I was told not to have sex for eight weeks, and to never wear tampons again. She also explained that I might have difficulty becoming pregnant, since scar tissue would develop in the area that was burned off. I was not having any sex, so this was not a concern. Two weeks later I walked across the stage to receive my diploma. I was in so much pain. Ben would ask if I was okay, and if I would be okay. I didn't share much, and replied with a simple, "Yes." I graduated, moved back to Chicago, and the relationship ended.

CHAPTER 8

MY NEW OLDER SISTER

The family sat around the table in my sister's apartment celebrating Christmas in 2004. I was twenty-one years old. My dad said he had to tell us something. His voice cracked, and I could see that he was nervous as he struggled with his words. I reached out to grab his hand to comfort him, I found that he was holding a photo. With my heart wide open, my ears alert, he told us that we had a sister named Liz. I never judged my father, as I always see the good in people. I was excited and open to this piece of information.

My dad fathered a child when he was eighteen years old. She lived in Mexico. Until that point, my sister and I had no idea that she existed. My brother had found out about her years before, but was asked to keep the secret to himself. My parents made a decision to not tell us about her. The reason my mother gave us for keeping the secret was that she was afraid that we too may want to become pregnant at a young age because our father had a child at a young age. I had a lot of questions, of course, but I had no ill feelings around my parents' decision. I looked at the picture my father had been holding of my new sister. She looked like me with gorgeous curly hair, but she was taller and darker. Although I didn't agree with my parents' decision to keep her from us, it went how it went. All of my father's family in Mexico, as well as my mother's father and mother had long-since known about her. They took the secret of my sister to the grave with them.

Fast-forward nine years later to October 2013: I decided to take a trip to Guadalajara to meet my half-sister. I was excited and open to the idea. At the fancy Rui Hotel in Guadalajara City, I finally got to meet Liz. As in the photo, she was tall, dark, and beautiful with the most gorgeous curly hair. We held each other tight. I told her I loved her, and that our lives would be forever changed by meeting each other. As it turns out, I also have a gorgeous niece named Mariana. We spent our time in Guadalajara enjoying each other, eating delectable food, and visiting Tlaquepaque. It was such a wonderful trip to get to meet the sister I did not know I had. She filled my heart. Our parents have their own stories, but Liz had only love and acceptance for me. The decisions our parents made were theirs. But now, we had the power to build our own amazing relationship. I try to visit Liz every year, and my hopes are that she will someday come to the U.S. to live with us.

After building the most loving relationship with Liz, the two of us had a conversation about things I had contemplated for many years. She had also thought about how this conversation would go. I wanted to know what she thought about her life. We had moved to the U.S., and she was left in Mexico. She knew of us, but we didn't know of her. She shared with me that she felt unworthy of being loved. This completely broke my heart, because she grew up wanting to know us and knew my father—her father—was in the U.S. with another family. She grew up with a lot of unanswered questions, just like I did. But we are very much alike. She understood that a decision was made to keep her a secret, and she had no control over it. Like my own, her childhood was a tough one. Neither of us judges, as we try to only see the good in others.

We are both compassionate, funny, loving, and enthusiastic about life. And as I mentioned before, we also look alike . . . we look like our dad. We adore and love each other as sisters should. She is extremely important to my life, and in the lives of my children.

My sister and I share blood, and I can feel the pain she experienced growing up without her father, knowing that he had another family. But we can't dwell on the past; all we have is the present. Even though we didn't agree with the decisions our parents made, we respect them, as much as they respect the decision of Liz and me to develop a wonderful relationship. My hope is that my sister's heart heals completely, and that she feels the love I have for her. My love is enough because I truly respect and admire her incredible strength. Her relationship with my father is also a special one in its own way. Time heals all wounds, and everything can be explored and resolved through conversation. I look forward to strengthening my special relationship with Liz for as long as we both are on this Earth.

CHAPTER 9

THE BROKEN SYSTEM

A s I sat in juvenile court, listening to all the judge's requests to parents, I thought to myself: *Let's hope they get their shit together.* Many times, I wanted the parents to fail because getting back their kids would not be in the kids' best interest. My job was to keep these defenseless angels safe from their mentally ill, alcoholic, drug-abusing, violent, possessive, and generally all-around fucked-up parents.

I landed a job at a non-profit organization in Logan Square, the Puerto Rican neighborhood of Chicago, as a case manager who dealt with children who were taken from their parents by the Department of Children & Family Services. It didn't pay much, but it was a great start. It seemed to align with the type of work I had been involved with back in college. My job was to support the kids and their parents with as many services as possible, with the desired end result of eventually reuniting the kids with their parents. It was a lot of work—long hours, tons of paperwork, and it was very heavy on the heart. I realized that the system was broken, and many kids were falling through the cracks. Children were being returned to their abusive homes when they should have been kept far away. The ones who did get removed were extreme cases. It was not only mentally and emotionally draining, but it was impossible to keep up with the case load, which never stopped growing. I didn't last long at this job, and left after six months with the painful feeling in my heart that this system would be broken forever.

Soon after, I picked up another case management job at another local Chicago non-profit organization working with the mentally ill population. I was assigned to work with mentally ill individuals who ended up receiving treatment in a state facility. I had never visited a state mental hospital. I had spent time in an outpatient mental health treatment facility while in high school, but this was different. The patients were highly medicated and zombie-like. We were assigned different cases. My job was to set them up with as many services as possible, such as food stamps, food vouchers, therapy sessions, and to coordinate their treatment plans. This was a very rewarding job because I felt that I was really making a difference in their lives. I also had the opportunity to run a counseling group at the state mental facility. One of my files was a lady who had experienced almost her entire family being murdered by a militia in her home country of Colombia. She and her daughter survived by hiding in the cupboards of their kitchen, and eventually gained asylum in the U.S. She had a brain stent due to a brain ailment she had suffered. She was very loving, kind, and giving.

Many of my patients were diagnosed with severe mental illnesses: psychotic disorders, schizophrenia, major depression, split personality disorder. You name it, they had it. I can't even begin to count the number of times I had to conduct an involuntary mental health admission to the state facility. One of my coworkers had been working on her master's degree and was going to be working fewer hours. She gifted me her files, which to me were the coolest and most interesting cases of all. She worked the cases that read "unfit to stand trial." These files were crazy, they were composed of murderers, rapists, and criminals with severe mental illness. Their conditions are so bad, they had been deemed "unfit to stand trial" or "not guilty due to insanity." These patients were housed in a super-locked-down mental health facility on the north side of Chicago. I read through some of the files: One guy had gotten upset with his boss and set him on fire; another had pushed his lover over a railing because the voices in his head told him to do it. These cases were captivating to me. These patients were even more medicated than usual, thus more zombie-like, to decrease their potential for danger.

I was going through a file of one of my patients, and was discussing with him his progress and crime. I was given a small button-looking necklace that we were to push if our safety was ever threatened. On this day, this patient seemed a little too bright-eyed for my comfort. He sat in front of me in a chair. I don't remember if it was something I said or did, but in a flash he reached out his arms, lunging towards me, wrapping his cracked hands around my neck, choking me. We both fell back on the chair. It happened so fast I didn't have time to process it. I remember his hot breath on my face and his teeth grinding together. Somehow, I was able to press my button to call for aid. Security rushed in and got him off me. His punishment, I was sure, would be solitary confinement, which was the absolute worst for this mentally ill population. Apparently, I had triggered him, and he was removed from my files. I thought to myself, *hmm, murderers need hugs too.* I was pretty unfazed by this; it was just another day on the job.

As case managers, it was our job to work with an entire team of mental health professionals to try to restore the sanity or mental fitness of our patients in order for them to be tried in court for their crimes. One case in particular was a young man who had tried to kill a young girl. His reason for grabbing her was because he liked her shiny bracelet. I went to his court hearing, walked through the door, and sat down. As the honorable judge came in, they announced her as Judge Lampkin. When I saw her and heard the name, chills ran down my spine. What a crazy world. Judge Lampkin had sentenced Emilio's sister's murderer to death. Judge Lampkin is a powerful woman with an incredible presence. She means business. The death penalty had not been given in many years until she received that case. In 2011, the Governor of Illinois abolished the death penalty, and the murderer of Emilio's sister remains in prison for life.

I had held on to a lot of anger after Emilio's sister's murder, but as I grew older and sat in many trials of Judge Lampkin, my own anger subsided. I always asked myself how she kept it together, listening to one insane crime after another. She was direct, strict, and a force to be reckoned with. I admired her presence, tenacity, and good will for justice. I wanted to be just like her. She is a badass.

This job was a great one, and I held it close and dear to my heart. I was exposed to so much and learned a lot about the severely mentally-ill population. After two years, I was ready to venture off into the world of investigations and undercover work.

CHAPTER 10

FLYING LOW, CRASHING FAST

During a high-speed chase through the mountains of upstate New York, I was the one being hunted. Trying to not lose control of my vehicle and plummet to my death, I managed to stay on the road and stay alive. I was an undercover surveillance agent working a corporate fraud case. This was an exciting new world for me. I was taught intensive background searching, how to impersonate someone else to gain access to valuable information, and spoof calling. Spoof calling is when you call someone and impersonate being someone else, and the caller ID matches where you claim to be calling from. For example, if we were calling your house from the courthouse, your caller ID would display the courthouse phone number. I became a master at obtaining information by all means possible, and learned how to investigate.

I was eventually thrown into the world of surveillance. I had never done surveillance before, and all the movies I had watched never prepared me for what I was about to experience. I had two bosses, and they were polar opposites. If one was day, the other was night. I had never worked with a boss who would practically lose his shit every other day. He would scream, throw things, and swear; he was like Bruce Banner turning into the Hulk. This behavior was a normal occurrence around our office. My other boss was calm, serene, and very chill. I guess this mixture worked. They were both masters of their craft. No one ever tells you how things will go doing undercover work. In reality, you basically learn on the job and make the best of it as you go. I was in my twenties, traveling to a different place each week, making a lot of money. The excitement, stress, and brain-releasing crazy hormones made the job intoxicating. I was thrown into the mix and became good at it very quickly.

No one ever trains you on how to use the bathroom when you're locked inside a surveillance van for hours on end. Of course, for guys, this is an easier task. But what about number two? We were often in surveillance vans for twelve or more hours and could not leave our position. Most of the male agents could easily pee in a bottle. But what about a woman? Well, as a female surveillance agent, you simply have to figure out how to survive and succeed in a male-dominant position. I did my business cat-style. I would buy a bucket, fill it with kitty litter, and presto . . . human litter box. Hey, it did the trick. The job was not easy at first. Learning to drive with one hand while holding a camera with the other was a skill that needed to be mastered with time. Keep in mind that this was old-school, stakeout-style surveillance. I got really good at that. Jumping from the back of the van to the front of the van in seconds was also a great skill to master. There was never a time when your heart wasn't jumping out of your chest. Surveillance today is a lot different. Most of it is done online, through social media, phone pings, GPS, and easy Facebook check-in bait. If you don't want to be tracked, easy—get off social media, stop checking in, and put your phone on airplane mode at all times. Today, everyone is so connected and attached to our electronic devices that we can be tracked much more easily. Your phone listens to you. Say "red shoes" out loud, then go to the search engine and type "red." The first search result that pops up will be "red shoes."

Of all the important training I learned on the job, the hardest skill to master was blending into the background and remaining unseen and unnoticed. We would follow our targets for days at a time without them ever knowing we were there. We lurked in the shadows, sat on the streets, highways, or in the bushes, always listening and always watching. Once, I made a hair appointment with one of the subjects of our investigation. I had a camera hidden in my bag. The subject dyed my hair as the camera sat right on the counter. Sadly, the camera defaulted and did not catch anything. This job made me super alert and aware of my surroundings. How was it possible that we could be following people and they would not notice? It goes to show how much people are unaware of what is happening around them. Now, more than ever, heads are always turned down looking down at phones; people are more vulnerable, distracted, and generally more disconnected from their surroundings.

Sometimes things did not go our way. Sometimes your cover would get blown, and it was not pretty. Sometimes we were shot at and chased. During one investigation in upstate New York, my cover was blown. The target turned and began chasing us. We called this the "cat and mouse game." The target chased me through the mountains of New York. These roads were icy, snowy, and uncharted for me, and I almost lost control of the van. The van came very close to the edge of the mountain. This chase left a psychological dent in me for sure. I definitely did not want to go out in an explosion caused by a car plummeting into the snowy abyss. In cases like this, the best course of action was to retreat and shut down the investigation. Investigations weren't shut down often, but they were sometimes.

They say that when you have a gun pointed at your face, you never forget the face of the person holding the gun. Your brain first scans the weapon, then moves up the arm and onto the face and meets the eyes. On one occasion, I had ten guns pointed at my head at once. When this happens, you don't move because any sudden movement most likely ends in your death. Obviously, because I am here telling you the story, I didn't move. I survived and was let go fairly unscathed; I was not raped or badly hurt. I never returned to those targets. Another agent had better luck and returned to finish the job that I was unable to. You would have thought that after an incident like this, I might want to take a break for a while. I brushed it off and kept going, completely emotionless to the ordeal. I do believe that being emotionally disconnected and unavailable allowed me to thrive in this field.

This work is how you earn your stripes. You do the crazy grunt work to be able to move up in the investigative world. Having surveillance undercover work under your belt not only makes you a badass, but gains you respect in investigative circles. But being a young, Hispanic woman elevates your street cred to a whole different level. There are very few women in male-dominant positions, especially Hispanic women. It is quite rare. Most women also don't do undercover work because, let's face it, it's not easy. No one ever wants to put their life on the line, but when they do, they are rewarded. Investigations are fascinating. There is always going to be something to uncover. No stone is ever left unturned. The cases are always different, with compelling people and stories. The work never dries up because money, drugs, secrets, and indecencies are a large part of what makes our world go around. Everything is fair game while trying to uncover the truth. For me, this job was a playground—a fast-paced, ever-changing, exciting, heart-pumping, incredible playground.

CHAPTER 11

PLAYING THE FIELD

Scrolling through the endless profiles on Myspace was like shopping for shoes. My job was stressful, dangerous, and exciting. Having your heart pump out of your chest from the fear of getting your cover blown was an intense feeling. I got to travel a lot, I had racked up so many air miles that my travel account resembled a Swiss bank account. To relieve the stress of my crazy experiences, I began to go out drinking. I was young, single, beautiful, and making a lot of money. At the time, my friend Jen had landed a job at a local radio station. Sophie, Jen, and I had VIP access anywhere we went because of Jen's job. I would travel for work on Sunday and return home on Friday. During this time, I made up for all the drinking and partying that I never did in my college days.

Emotionally unavailable, arrogance running high, and with no intentions of having any type of commitment, I began playing the field. I had not dated in a long time. At the time, Myspace was the most popular social media outlet. Meeting guys on Myspace was easy since you could scroll through endless profiles. One night while scrolling through profiles, I found a good-looking, green-eyed, half-Italian, half-Puerto Rican guy named Alex. I sent him a message, and he responded quickly. He lived in the South side and told me he was getting ready to leave for Marine bootcamp. He still wanted to hang out and get to know me. We met at a Denny's, went back to his house, and hung out. He was incredibly attractive and very sweet. At the time, he was living with his father, a retired Chicago cop, and a cute little white Maltese named Semper Fi. We hit it off, and he promised he would write letters from bootcamp. Two weeks later he was off to Camp Pendleton. To my surprise, his letters began arriving. We continued to write to each other for the entirety of his boot camp experience. It was romantic . . . old-school romantic.

In writing, we talked about the possibility of me going to San Diego to visit him. We had grown so close through our letters that I decided to make the trip. I drove to the South Side of Chicago to meet up with his father and pick up some items that he wanted to send along for his son. His father had bright eyes and a friendly smile. The two resembled each other. His father said to me, "Thank you for going to visit my son." We had a blast in San Diego, but because of his stringent bootcamp schedule, we got to spend only one day together. I flew back, and we continued writing letters. Since he was in San Diego and in the military, I kept my options open.

I met another handsome Puerto Rican, Fernando, who at the time was singing in a boy band and working in financial services. He was a rather good singer, and a real "playa." He was driven and passionate. He was independent, financially stable, and had big dreams. Our time together was short-lived and fun. I kept him a secret. We had a lot in common because we were both all about success. We had established that our relationship would be strictly physical. He mentioned how he wanted to work in radio. I told him that my friend Jen worked in radio, and that she had worked herself up the ladder. He was highly motivated and went back to school to get a communications degree. He worked himself up to being a top DJ for a popular Chicago radio station. Every time I go to Chicago, I hear his voice through the radio.

The music was blaring, the drinks were flowing, and the crowd was lit. Through the corner of my eye, I saw my cousin Juana. I was so excited very see her, and we exchanged numbers and promised to hang out. That night I saw some old friends from high school, and a tall, dark, and handsome guy caught my eye. I asked my friend who he was. I had never seen him before. My friend was surprised that I was interested. I told my friend to give Tall, Dark, and Handsome my phone number.

My cousin Juana and I began hanging out often, painting the town red whenever the opportunity presented itself. We grew close like sisters. She was full of life, gorgeous, and so much fun. She was and still is a very accomplished hairdresser. She was there for me and always made sure I looked my best. We spent a lot of valuable time together, and went through our ups and downs trying to navigate life in our twenties. Sometimes we had too much fun. We were drinking and partying regularly until the early hours of the morning. Sophie, Jen, and Juana blended perfectly into the Chicago nightlife scene, leading us to meet many celebrities, professional athletes (including Michael Jordan), and a certain massively popular reggaeton singer who will remain anonymous. He called me every time he was in town, but I was already hooked on someone else.

Tall, Dark, and Handsome's name was Sebastian. He eventually called, and we began talking. He was an Army veteran who worked for the Transportation Security Administration (TSA). He had ridiculous confidence. We hung out once and were quickly hooked on each other. I believe that we were both emotionally unavailable, but our chemistry was undeniable. Until Sebastian, I never had so much chemistry with someone I barely knew. We were very attracted to each other, and he was very passionate. We talked often and grew close. The emotional connection was present, even though I tried to convince myself that our relationship was purely physical. He was not ready to commit, and I wasn't either. But when I would get drunk, he would receive the drunken call asking when we were going to make things official. We had a lot of fun, and on those lonely nights, I called him, and he called me. We kept our relationship on the down low and no one really knew the extent of it. My cousin Juana and Sophie knew that the two of us were involved. Juana said that I should just move on because nothing would ever come of the relationship. We kept in touch throughout the years, and we had a lot in common. He had big dreams and was a hard worker. He went on to become a highly successful federal agent. We managed to reconnect in 2009 and again in 2021. I was already living in Houston and had ended an abusive relationship. We talked and texted often, but we both knew that our time had passed. We always maintained the best intentions for each other, and always wished each other well.

During the period of time that Sebastian and I were talking, Alex's father became ill and needed a kidney transplant. Alex was honorably discharged from the Marines and gifted his father a kidney, saving his life. I sent him a teddy bear and flowers when he was discharged from the hospital. Once he recovered, we went out on the town in hopes of not messing up his one remaining kidney. We drank heavily and came back to my place. Weeks later, Juana and I were at Sophie's posh Lincoln Park apartment, and I told them that I had not gotten my period. Sophie asked if there was a possibility that I could be pregnant. I shrugged. Sophie happened to have a pregnancy test with her, and handed it to me. I took the test, and it showed positive. My heart sank. I was frightened. Our eyes were wide with surprise. We decided to go out that night to try to lessen the shock. I did not drink that night, and my mind would not stop racing. I could not have this baby. I was in the midst of building my career; Alex had just left the marines—we were young and not ready for a baby. I chose to not tell him. I had always been pro-life, but when I was placed in the situation of making this decision for myself, I decided to have an abortion.

I was young, just beginning my career, and working my way up. Having this baby would be a curveball. I was traveling all over doing undercover work, and this baby would end all that. I called my sister and explained the situation. She took me to the abortion clinic. I cried so much because I was not fully committed to my decision. As they put the anesthesia mask over my face, tears rolled down my cheeks. The last thing I remember is the nurse saying, "It is going to be okay." I woke up and it was over. My sister took me home, and I lay in bed for what seemed like an eternity. Having an abortion was not an easy decision. In fact, having to make this decision changed me in many ways. I stopped going out, drinking, and partying. It all stopped. I cut out many people from my life, including Sebastian. I was ashamed, embarrassed, regretful, and felt alone. I had sleepless nights and regretted my decision. Despite my pain, I continued working undercover. Alex and I were no longer dating and had no plans of being in a relationship. He was rebuilding his life after coming out of the Marines. Years later I told him about the baby. He was surprised but understood. He agreed that we were young and that he too would have made the same decision. Alex is now a successful Chicago cop.

CHAPTER 12

BROKEN PIECES

One night while out with Juana and Sophie, I met an adorable guy from Milwaukee. He had the most captivating dimples. Chris was quiet, sweet, and shy. We exchanged numbers and began to talk. He didn't know anything about me, so it was a fresh start. I confided in him and told him that I previously had an abortion. He didn't judge me, and simply listened. Because he was in Milwaukee, we talked a lot and for long hours. We started a long-distance relationship. I was not a fan of long-distance relationships since my last one did not turn out too well. My partying ways and late-night hookups with Sebastian had been over. I had been too sad and ashamed to even tell him what happened. I started to notice that I went from relationship to relationship without a break. My inability to be alone was an issue.

Chris came from a great family. I grew close with them, especially his mother. She was a beautiful school principal, highly intelligent, and super classy. His father was an electrician and owned his own company. His parents were divorced and had been for a while. Looking back now, I don't think I ever loved him. I think I fell in love with the idea of us. I do believe the long distance played into the mystery and idealization of the relationship. Chris insisted that we move in together. Since we got to see each other only two weekends out of the month, I would visit him in Milwaukee, and he would visit me. All my friends were not very sure about Chris. He was somewhat antisocial, and really loosened up only when he drank. He moved into my condo fairly quickly, which left people wondering about his intentions.

Chris was a great listener, and I do believe he helped me heal the pain I felt following the abortion. When he moved in, he was highly motivated. He landed a job and started attending electrical school. He went to school in the mornings and worked nights, so we never saw each other. By the time he came home close to midnight, I was long asleep. We just saw each other in passing, only really spending our weekends together. The relationship was far from perfect. We would have bad fights and make up, just to fight again. Insecurity and lies were features of our relationship. When the opportunity arose for me to move to Houston to expand my career, he jumped right on it. I was not as excited. In fact, I didn't even like Houston, but he convinced me that it would be amazing and that we could live a life together.

The week before we moved to Houston, his family threw us a going-away party in Milwaukee. Everyone was having a great time, drinking, and eating. It was late and I wanted to go home, so I told Chris I was heading back to his mother's house. Chris wanted to stay longer and hang out with his friends. He came to his mother's home extremely drunk. I was already in bed, and he turned on the light. He was upset because I had left and not stayed. He grabbed me from the bed and threw me against the wall. I pushed him back. I called his sister, got in my car, and drove all the way back to Chicago, leaving him behind. I was ready to be done with him. The relationship had become very toxic, but he would always convince me to stay. So, the following day, I returned to Milwaukee to pick him up.

There would be other instances when we would fight, break up, and he would leave—just to come back again. The day for our move to Houston arrived. It was July of 2008. I was going to start working immediately on human trafficking cases. Houston is the number one city for human trafficking in the U.S. We were in a new city with no friends and hanging out only with my parents. I told him I wanted to make friends and bought myself a membership to the local gym. He did not like the idea of me going to the gym, or even that I wanted to make friends for that matter. He wanted it to only be us. He became possessive and aggressive. He had difficulty finding a job, and when I came home from work he would often still be sitting on the same spot on the couch where he was when I left. He would drink and get obnoxious and annoying. I fell out of love with him fast. I wanted out, but I didn't know how to end the relationship.

At the gym, I met a gorgeous blonde trainer named Emme. She was very sweet and nice. Emme became my first friend in Houston. I called her Fitness Barbie, because she looked like a Barbie Doll. Chris had finally landed a job, but I had already checked out of the relationship. My eyes started wandering, and they wandered fast. I saw an incredibly fit, gorgeous trainer at the gym. Isaiah was forty at the time, and I was twenty-seven. I was so interested in him, and what I had going on at home was so sour, that seeing him made me forget it all. I confided in Emme, and she became aware of my newfound happiness. Chris was so busy with his new job that he didn't even realize how much time I was spending at the gym. I ended up switching up my trainers and hired Isaiah.

We began training and flirting heavily. Isaiah was ridiculously attractive; he had an eight-pack and looked like he was created by Michelangelo. He was sweet, funny, older, and so confident. We grew close, and he knew my situation at home. It didn't seem to bother him. The sexual tension between us grew and grew. I would see him three times a week per our training schedule, and text like crazy in between. One week, Chris went to Dallas for training. I didn't even think twice. I went to spend the week with Isaiah at his apartment. All that sexual tension that built up over the past two months was released to the sounds of *808s & Heartbreak* by Kanye West.

By December of 2008, merely six months after moving to Houston, the relationship with Chris was officially over. I called Sophie in Chicago and told her what had happened. Sophie told me, "Okay, it's time for you to end it. Cut him loose and let him go back to Milwaukee to be with his family for Christmas." When Chris came home from Dallas, he knew something was not right. I finally just told him, "I don't love you anymore, and I want this relationship to be over. I want you to leave." The conversation escalated, and he became desperate, angry, and then sad. He kept asking me if there was someone else. I lied and told him no. I told Chris I didn't see a future with him, and this relationship would not work. He pleaded with me. He said he would stop drinking. He became so mad that he punched a hole into a wall. I told him that he could remain in the house until he found a stable place, but he grabbed his clothes and his extensive shoe collection and was gone.

For some time, Chris believed I would call him to come back, since this happened to be a common occurrence during the two years we had spent together. With Chris gone, I could now spend more time with Isaiah. A couple of days after Chris left, my neighbor called to tell me that Chris had spent the night in front of the house waiting for me to come home. This was crazy and scary. Chris would "blow up" my phone and was angry that I had not been home. He asked who I was with. He was so upset that I feared for my safety. My mother called him and lied to him, saying that that I had spent the night with her. I had been with Isaiah. It took about a month to have Chris stop popping up. But as he lingered, I became pregnant again. This time it was not a drunken night, but rather, a ripped condom.

Once again, I was back to the same place I had been two years prior. Isaiah was already a father of two, and much older than me. I didn't see a future with him, and I knew our relationship had been an escape from Chris. I called Sophie to tell her the news. I was now financially stable, working a great job, and living in a new home. Sophie thought I should keep the baby. Isaiah was open to having the baby and raising it together. He told me, "I will not marry you, but I will raise this baby with you." He was extremely supportive of whatever I decided. Again, while torn about the decision to have an abortion or not, my sister came to town. I decided to abort the fetus. Isaiah supported my decision, and I made an appointment to go to the clinic with my sister. But this time, as soon as we got to the clinic I turned around and walked back out.

CHAPTER 13

FROM TOXIC TO DEADLY

My sister had to go back to Chicago, and I decided to tell my mother about the pregnancy. Never in a million years would I have thought that I would be calling my mother to tell her that I was pregnant with the baby of a man whom I did not plan on being with. Even though Isaiah and I had a lot of fun, we were in totally different stages of our lives. I never planned on being in a relationship with him. He had been, for the most part, nothing more than a gorgeous distraction. To my surprise, my mother supported me, held me tight, and did not judge me. She asked me what I wanted to do. I told her I did not want to keep the baby. This time around the decision was clear, but still, it hurt no less. My mother drove me to the clinic, hugged me, and told me it would all be okay. What are the odds that I would get pregnant again while using a condom? Well, it does happen. After the abortion, the relationship between Isaiah and myself was more or less over. That flamed burned strongly, but it died out even faster. I continued to see him at the gym, and he began to grow jealous and insecure about the fact that we weren't going to stay together. Chris was out of the picture, and soon Isaiah would be too.

Emme and I were young, single, and always ready to mingle. Looking back, I was very misguided about my own insecurities trying to make it in the male-dominant government world. I was starting to rise to the top, ranking as one of the best investigators/interrogators in Houston. But being a woman in a male-dominant field meant that you were always an easy target for demotion. My career success meant that I experienced a lot of pushback from the male investigators. In government work, the great rise to the top fast—and everyone wants a spot at the top. I vowed to myself that I would never date anyone I was working with in any capacity. I valued my career and wanted a clear path forward for it. I did not want to mix business and pleasure. I worked with many good-looking men, but most were huge players, married, and cheating. I stayed away.

One night, Emme and I went out on the town. A dimple-faced, super-fit Hispanic guy caught my eye. I had been drinking, so I went up to him and introduced myself. He said he was a teacher, and that it was his birthday. We exchanged numbers. Little did I know this would be the relationship that would finally break me. Eric talked a big game, was charming, confident, and exciting. He was a triathlete and in great shape, and he was also modeling at the time. Since I was coming out of two failed relationships, he seemed like a good distraction. I didn't plan on being in a relationship with him; I just intended to hang out. I was wrong. This relationship moved quickly. He was very insecure and possessive. He had an exaggerated sense of self-importance and talked up his achievements and success. But in reality, he was broke and in ridiculous debt. He talked about finding his soul mate, and swore I was it.

For some time, I believed him, and we did become very much enmeshed with each other. I started listening to the music he listened to, running, biking, swimming, and even eating at his favorite restaurants. I was caught up in his narcissistic web. He was a sex addict, not just with me, but with everyone else. During the course of our relationship, I became so hypnotized by his bullshit that I didn't want to believe it. Part of me knew that he was never faithful, and that he was cheating on me—not just with other girls, but with guys too. Until this day he will deny all of this. I take responsibility for my own participation in the relationship, because, what does it say about me dating someone as narcissistic and fucked up as him? I was insecure, lost, and broken. I was not a sex addict; I was a love addict. I was someone who was incapable of being alone, who jumped from relationship to relationship, and who idealized the perfect relationship. I chose one wrong partner after the next, usually having one foot in one relationship and one in another.

During my relationship with Eric, I became obsessed with triathlons. I bought all the gear—his and mine—including buying him two bikes, food, clothes, trips, hotels, race entries, and even a car. I even paid for him to get his U.S. citizenship. I was very financially stable, and Eric had me wrapped around his narcissistic finger. He had a deep need for excessive attention, admiration, and was extremely vain. When we would fight, it was insane. He would say I was a piece of shit, that no one would ever want me, and swore that I would never find anyone better than him. This I later learned is called gaslighting—a form of manipulation and extreme emotional abuse with the perpetrator creating a distorted reality. Every time I tried to leave, he would pull me back in by saying we were meant for each other and that we were soul mates. One day, he called to tell me that we should go down to the courthouse and get married. He always wanted to move into my home, and had even begun moving his stuff into my place. In the course of all this madness with Eric is when I met Gabrielle.

As I scurried to get on the boat at the Gateway to the Bay Triathlon in Kemah, TX (an Olympic distance), trying to zip up my wetsuit, a bright-eyed, friendly, smiling lady came up to me to ask if I needed help. I said yes. Meeting Gabrielle saved my life. We quickly became friends. She was involved in a non-profit organization that was raising funds for youth in at-risk environments. She invited me to be on her fundraising team. Gabrielle and I became close. She saw the ridiculous relationship that I was in with Eric. She saw how we would fight and break up, only to get back together, even after I swore it was over. One day I called Eric to tell him to drop off the car I had bought for him, and that if he didn't, I would call the cops. He parked the car in front of my home and left. I grabbed a jug of gasoline, held it in my hand, and was going to blow up the car. I called Gabrielle and told her, "I am going to blow up this car." Gabrielle and her husband came immediately and took the car away.

It was time for me to get out of this toxic relationship; it had rotted me from the inside out. I called Eric and told him, "One day you will not have control over me, and we will be over." He swore that I would always belong to him. Even his own best friend, Joel, had told me that Eric had always been cheating on me. Eric, upset that his own best friend had betrayed him, kicked Joel out of their apartment. I felt horrible for Joel, but I was too caught up in the bullshit to leave Eric. Years later, I ran into Joel at a New Year's party. I went up to him and apologized for throwing him under the bus. Joel accepted my apology, and we began what would become a wonderful friendship. Joel was even present at my wedding.

I was introduced to a program called Sex and Love Addicts Anonymous (SLAA), a twelve-step program just like Alcoholics Anonymous. I was also given Pia Mellody's book, *Facing Love Addiction*. I read it in only two days, and everything in it seemed to be written especially for me. I went to a meeting and sat quietly, listening. As I heard the numerous stories from other women, I knew this group was a place I belonged. I had mistaken intense sexual experiences with the new romantic excitement of love. I would skip directly over any emotional connection and only allow for the physical to dictate the direction. It is extremely common for women to feel this in new relationships. I constantly wanted a romantic relationship, and feared being alone. I would choose partners who were emotionally unavailable, or verbally and physically abusive, and then find it difficult or impossible to leave the unhealthy and abusive relationship.

CHAPTER 14

REBIRTH

After finally ending my horrible relationship with Eric, I committed to the SLAA program. I found an incredible sponsor, Mary, who was a real hard-ass. She was an elderly business owner who had been recovering from love addiction for over twenty-five years. I worked through the program and was able to detach myself completely from Eric. Although he continued trying to reel me back in, I had grown confident. A newfound rebirth was taking place. I had lost my identity in him; I didn't even know who I was anymore. This relationship had been so extremely painful for me that it destroyed me. Ultimately, I am glad that it did, because then I was able to rebuild myself. I became a woman I could love again—a woman I could learn to take care of. I had to date myself, find myself, and learn to be alone. I had not been alone since college, and after so many failed relationships, I needed to heal.

In the midst of my recovery, I had been training for my first Ironman Triathlon—a 2.4-mile swim, 112-mile bike ride, and 26.22-mile run. I had thrown all my time and effort into training and SLAA. Those were my two priorities. I completed my first Ironman Triathlon in May of 2011. It was a mentally and physically draining journey in which most of my training had been completed in the middle of a toxic relationship. I saw Eric on the Ironman course and at the finish line. He lingered as I celebrated with my family and friends. It was stalkerish, but I was so far removed from him that it didn't matter. My life without him had grown amazing. I had worked the program and had even rescued the cutest blue-eyed Australian Shepherd mix whom I named Tri. Tri was my furry guardian. We would spend nights and weekends hanging out on the couch with no one else around. That dog was my everything. I did not want to date at all. Being single and alone had become an amazing experience. I had learned to love myself and my loneliness. It was soothing and wonderful. I knew I eventually wanted to attempt dating again, get married, and have children. But for a whole year I only dated myself, stayed celibate, trained, and worked my program.

My sponsor Mary called me one day and said, "You are not going to find a husband sitting at home with your dog." Mary, and the SLAA program, had taught me so much about relationships and the importance of building an emotional connection. Mary would also talk about the three-month rule. When you get a new job, you do not get benefits for three months until you prove yourself to be worthy of them. I loved how this translated into the world of relationships. In the past, I had been driven by physical attraction, and building an emotional connection came last. It was time to date, and it was time for an extremely strict dating plan. The plan was easy: One date per week on a weekday, never on a weekend; no crazy texting and no texting after 10 p.m.; no kissing; no sex; no physical intimacy until the commitment and emotional connection had been established. Easy enough, right? The most important thing I had learned from SLAA was that love and being in a relationship was a choice. Happiness is a choice. A partner's purpose is not to make you happy or feel good about yourself. Love is something we choose. Building an emotional connection is the basis for any healthy relationship.

I asked Mary, "Where am I supposed to find guys to date if I don't go out or drink?" She said, "Match.com." I set up a free trial account on Match.com, and off I went. I told Mary I would not respond to anyone who made compliments about my physical appearance. I deleted any message that went down that road. I went on two dates. The first guy was an asshole, just like my ex. I was still picking assholes. The second guy was my future husband.

I received a message from a dark-haired, dark-eyed, great-looking Cuban guy who went by Ray. He was different from the guys I was used to going after. He had a kind smile. He sent me a message complimenting my passions and ambitions, which caught my attention. We spoke on the phone before we went out. I told him I had strict rules. I was trying to build an emotional connection, get married, and have kids—no "BS." At first, he thought I might be too stringent for his taste. But we decided to go out for a sushi dinner.

CHAPTER 15

FINALLY, TRUE LOVE

I arrived at the sushi restaurant with my music blaring. Ray arrived in a nice BMW. Could it be that I was finally going to be dating someone who was as financially stable as I was? To my surprise, his Match.com picture did not do him justice. He was much better looking in person. His real name was Ramon. We had a substantial conversation, and there was chemistry between us. I thought he was perfect in every way, except for his hairy arms. But I could look past that. After the first date, I told myself that I was going to marry him. I even called Gabrielle and told her the same thing. She thought I was crazy.

Now it was my time to exercise my dating plan, and I would do everything Mary had told me to do: No kissing, no sex, and only seeing him once a week on a weekday. We talked and texted often, and the conversation was always interesting. He was very interested in my job and thought it was awesome. This is why I thought he did not have anything crazy to hide. In fact, my husband is the only man I did not do a background check on; he never gave me a reason to. He was kind, loving, attentive, sweet, great to look at, and he smiled with his eyes. He was aware of my rules. Ray was and is an extremely good-looking man and was used to getting any girl he wanted. Well, this woman was not going to put out that easily. On the second date he tried to kiss me, and I turned my head.

I do think he enjoyed the chase, and it caused him to want me even more. As our relationship blossomed, we began to establish an emotional connection. I told him there would be no intimacy until we both decided that we were going to be in an exclusive relationship. He said he would wait for me to tell him when.

Ray and I met in July of 2011. During the first week we were dating, I was completing the Landmark Forum course that Gabrielle told me to attend. Landmark is a three-day self-development course that allows you to build a life that you get to be the author of. I would leave the Landmark class, and Ray and I would talk about anything that had come up for me during the day. Ray has always been obsessed with Asian food, so most of the dates were in Asian, especially Vietnamese, restaurants. Our emotional connection was growing.

In September of 2011, I left for Chicago and could not stop thinking of him. He had already written me a letter telling me how much he loved my smile, my attitude, my demeanor, and therefore . . . he loved me. I told my family about him and was ready to make a commitment. I was scared but excited. When I returned from Chicago, I told him I was ready to commit. He was excited; we were both very much in love. We had built an amazing emotional connection—a connection I had never experienced before, and it was purely and meticulously formed. On the fourth month of us dating, Ray managed to ask my parents for my hand in marriage, purchase a Tacori ring, and keep this all from the best investigator in Houston, Texas. Four months into our relationship, he put a ring on it.

It was the morning of December 31, 2011, and I was woken up by Tri's wet nose in my face. As I awoke and looked up, a ring box was hanging from his neck. I looked at Ray and said, "Are you serious? Is this really happening?" He grabbed the box, opened it, took a knee, and asked me to marry him. Not only had he done all that without me knowing, but he had also planned a getaway trip to celebrate. He whisked me away to the nicest cabin in all of Texas Hill Country. I was so happy, my face hurt from smiling. We were engaged for two years and got married in the most gorgeous Spanish-style wedding in March of 2013.

I believe Ray and I were meant to be together. I believe in life we have several soul mates, but we must find only one. Ray and I met on Match.com, but as we got to know each other, we discovered that we had the craziest coincidences. Ray worked with my triathlon friend, Claudia, but she never thought about introducing us. In fact, a week after Ray and I met, he was scheduled to be at a triathlon that I was racing, volunteering with the non-profit that I was racing with. Claudia would have been bringing Ray to the triathlon, so if we did not meet on Match.com, we would have met at the triathlon anyway. Two weeks after that, Ray's stepfather had finished building my friend Sandra's restaurant. Ray was invited to the restaurant on opening day. I would have met Ray there, too, if we had not met on Match. This was crazy to me. This is the primary example of why I believe that the universe aligns in a certain way, and that things just fall into place.

Both of our careers were taking off, and we had just built a custom Spanish-style home. Ray works in commercial real estate and made the leap from a salaried position to one that was fully commission-based. I began to travel more with work, and work was starting to get more intense. I would be working more internal affairs cases, and really got deep into my interrogation mastery.

Ray knew that I was obsessed with travel, and he embraced it. In the first few months we dated, we traveled to Austin, Dallas, and Arizona. We also took some amazing trips before having our babies. What was supposed to be a low-key honeymoon in Costa Rica turned into an all-out adventure with white water rafting, rappeling, and canoeing through the jungles of the Arenal Volcano. We also took an incredible ten-day tour of the entire country of Peru, going from Lima, to Arequipa, to climbing Colca Canyon, to sight-seeing in Puno and the floating Uros islands, and, of course, trekking up glorious Machu Picchu. We even got to live with an indigenous family in Taquile Island near the Uros floating islands on Lake Titicaca. Peruvians climb mountains at a crazy elevation wearing sandals. The women literally give birth, and the next day are back to working the land with their new babies wrapped in a cloth around them. But the most interesting aspects of these incredible people are their beliefs. They believe that a man should master the art of belt-making in order to be considered ready for marriage. They also allow a two-year trial period where couples live with each other before committing. If the trial period goes well, then you marry. This trial period obviously includes sexual intimacy. I thought this was extremely bold and smart. Peru, by far, was the coolest trip we had ever taken. It was all the adventure we needed before we started a family.

CHAPTER 16

IRONMAN ADVENTURES

I was still deep in the world of triathlons, and Ray was my number one fan. But eventually he got tired of being my cheerleader, and decided he was going to race too. He was super fit and had been a collegiate baseball player. He did well in triathlons and was ridiculously fast on the run. We went to Dallas for an Olympic triathlon as a three-person team. I would swim, Gabrielle would bike, and Ray would run. I was a fast swimmer and demolished the competition in my segment. Gabrielle rode hard, and Ray brought us home. Ray ran a six-and-a-half-minute average ten-miler in Vibram FiveFingers shoes. These were minimalist shoes with barely any support that are supposed to mimic running barefoot. We ended up placing second and taking home some serious hardware, including extra funds for the charity Cherish Our Children International (COCI), of which I was the fundraising team lead. The Rockwall Olympic Triathlon had become our race, and we raced there for two years.

In November of 2013, about thirty of us traveled to Cozumel, Mexico, to watch twenty-five or so of our friends compete in Ironman Cozumel. That year, there was a whirlpool in the ocean that about two hundred athletes got caught in. Athletes got stuck in the whirlpool, unable to escape it, and were not making the two-hour cut-off time for the 2.4-mile swim. Imagine being around a bunch of triathletes and all they talked about was racing, gear, food, and race times. It must have been annoying for Ray. But we were celebrating mine and Ray's thirtieth birthdays in beautiful Cozumel. We had a blast.

Two years prior, in 2011, I was racing my second Ironman Triathlon in Tempe, Arizona. I had meticulously trained and had hired a whole team to make sure I crushed this competition. I had a nutritionist, a triathlon coach, a swim coach, and ran complete running and cycling endurance tests. I knew exactly when my body would hit a wall. My nutrition was on point, and I knew how to fuel my body for this long and difficult race. I bought a custom-built CEEPO carbon bike with all carbon wheels that costs $8,000. This was supposed to be my stellar Ironman performance. Ironman Arizona was a fairly flat and fast course. The run had many ups and downs and turns. I was ready for an all-time personal best performance. When you train for an Ironman race, your entire life is based on training, sleeping, and fueling your body. You buy ridiculous amounts of gear, and it is an extreme hobby to be involved in. All my friends at the time were involved with triathlons, and all they did was train, eat, and talk about what race we were signing up for next.

You train for six to twelve months to complete an Ironman race. It is not easy, but it is possible. As long as you train and focus on fueling (what you eat before and during the race) you will be okay. Well, on this day I would be tested not just physically but mentally. I had a good swim and a good bike. My mental strength would be tested when I arrived at the run. On mile ten of the marathon, I rolled my left ankle on a small rock. It hurt like hell, but since I was so engrossed in the race, everything hurt at that point. I knew I had sprained my ankle. I looked down and saw that my left ankle had turned purple, almost black. The pain began to radiate up my calf. Something was seriously wrong, but I didn't come this far to quit—there is no quit in me. I kept moving. I was no longer running but walking fast. When I got to mile thirteen, I saw Gabrielle and Ray. I told Gabrielle I had hurt my foot, and it hurt like hell. Gabrielle said, "Keep moving, one foot in front of the other." We convinced ourselves that the purple-black we saw coming out of my sock was dirt. My ankle was swollen and enlarged. Gabrielle and Ray ended up walking practically thirteen miles with me on the entire marathon course. Never in my mind did I think I would be one of the last people to finish the race. This humbled me.

The pain was excruciating, but when you commit to finishing a race, your mind takes you to a whole new dimension. I zoned out from the pain and kept moving. I knew something was not right, but with Gabrielle and Ray by my side, I kept moving. I can't even count how many times I told Gabrielle I wanted to stop. She did not let me stop. She was not going to let me quit. I had trained so hard and long that I was determined to cross this finish line before the clock ran out. Thinking back, I have no idea how I pushed through the pain, but our mind is a powerful tool. Your mind can take you to places you did not even know existed. Mind over matter is a real phenomenon.

The energy at an Ironman finish line is electric; it is like a shot of life that moves through you. Everyone gathers at the finish line to welcome the last people who have been out on the course for over sixteen hours. The cutoff time for an Ironman race is seventeen hours. Do you know what it is like to have your body be in motion for over sixteen hours? It is excruciating. The loud cheers, the people, the music, and the crowd are intoxicating. This is why Ironman competitions are addictive. Running through the finish line feels like a drug to your brain. That final one-minute run to the finish line is why Ironman athletes sign up for their next race. They forget about all the pain they endured up until that point.

As I saw the finish line, I felt a wave of new energy. I do not know where the hell it comes from, but I am going to guess it is a huge shot of adrenaline that stimulates your brain, and you become untouchable. I crossed the Ironman finish line with only minutes left on the clock. There is a video on YouTube of the last minutes of Ironman Arizona 2011 where I'm seen running towards the finish line. As I crossed the finish line, I collapsed. I did not walk away; I was wheeled away. I had ripped all the ligaments and tendons in my left ankle. Obviously, we didn't find this out until I got back home and had X-rays and MRIs conducted. I left Arizona with a new shiny medal, a second Ironman title . . . and two shiny new crutches. I underwent a full left ankle reconstructive surgery, which was conducted by my fellow Ironman friend Dr. Randy Beckman. After surgery, he said the surgery was badly needed. After a fancy boot and some intense rehab, I was once again like new. With a new, tight ankle that needed to be loosened, I decided to try out trail running next.

CHAPTER 17

THE UGLY REALITY

Money makes the world go round, and as long as there is money involved, crime, drug dealing, human trafficking, and terrorism will never end. Working active human trafficking and drug-dealing cases has brought me a whole new awareness of the world. You can never judge a person by their looks because you do not know their journey, their story. People engage in all types of unsavory acts for many different reasons. I've learned that children get sold off to human traffickers for money—money that is needed to feed either other children or an extended family. Sacrifice one child to save four is the reasoning. Sometimes money just seems a better option than having to deal with a child or an adolescent.

The age range that is most sought out is nine to eleven. At this age, girls are still girls, and have not yet developed. Once they have developed, they are no longer good enough for a pedophile. It is a sick, dark, sad world, but it is reality. I mentioned earlier that Houston has the highest human trafficking rates in the country. One thing that many people don't know is that not all trafficked children are undocumented immigrants. In actuality, it is a combination of undocumented children who were sold off by their own parents, children who are abandoned, or even kidnapped for having a "specific look." Yes, even attractive or culturally ambiguous children are ones that are sought-after. Just like a good-quality drink, there are good quality children. Addiction comes with many different monster heads, but most have the same outcome. You pursue what you're addicted to in order to satisfy an urge or to fill a void, but you are never satisfied. The more you get, the more you want. Since the COVID-19 pandemic hit, people's addictions and vices have come out to play even harder. In times of stress, your drug of choice is what alleviates the pain, be it drugs, sex, alcohol, shopping, gambling . . . even murder.

People like to think of pedophiles as bad, broken, unsuccessful, alcoholic, etc. But in reality, they can be CEOS, executives, pastors, or your neighbor—they are regular-looking and highly functioning individuals. Have you ever seen the show To Catch a Predator? The people featured often hold high positions, have huge responsibilities, and are phenomenally successful. Addiction is powerful, and it sinks its teeth into your very being. It is hard to shake, and even harder to control. Sobriety in its purest form is also hard to sustain and maintain.

The children of trafficking are usually led to believe that being trafficked is their calling, that it is okay, and that this is a lucrative form of making-money. Many girls grow up believing that this is how they are shown love, affection, and connection. Although many trafficked children are prisoners, their captors convince them this is a lifestyle that they belong in. Many of these girls do not know what love is, or how it is supposed to look. In many cases, their own families sold them off, so how could they possibly know that it is wrong? When speaking with these girls, it is clear they are lost in a misconstrued reality. At some point they go numb and stop feeling anything. It also happens to the people who interview them . . . people like me. Their captors are also highly functioning, professional individuals who are using the girls to make residual income on the side. The sale of humans is a massive money-making market, and unfortunately, just like drugs, as long as there is someone ready and willing to pay for it, it will never end.

While human trafficking is a huge problem, another major problem is drug trafficking.. Drugs come at a huge price. The closer you are to the border, the lower the cost of the drug, so the cost of drugs is really based on the distance it needs to travel. The border is packed with agents, dogs, and security, but unfortunately, money talks. Officials are paid off, and drugs enter the country via people, vehicles, boats, and planes. Our own military has even allowed drugs to be smuggled into our country. At the right price, anyone will be willing to turn their heads for a second. A kilo of high-quality coke is 2.2 pounds, and the best coke will sell for $38,000 a kilo. There are 16 ounces in a pound, so that equates to about $1,000 for 1 ounce. Transactions being made from huge drug cartels are in the millions of dollars. Good drugs come at a high price, and there are people willing to pay that high price, whether it be cocaine, meth, heroin, ecstasy, or other man-made lab pills. Making meth is a long, drawn-out process that takes time, effort, and a lot of preparation. Cooks that make meth usually do not live long because of the inhalation of all the chemicals that go into the product. Pills have gotten extremely popular among younger crowds, and because they are cheaper, addiction has become deadlier. The more addictive the drugs, the better it is for business, because as long as there is addiction, there will be demand. Pills can be the deadliest drug because they are usually made with all types of crazy chemicals in a bathtub in China. The chemicals eat away at your brain. They make your brain want more, your tolerance goes up, your brain craves more, and eventually an overdose occurs.

The people who sell and run these drugs all around the country are motivated by the money, which you discover after interviewing many of the "runners." These people have families, and children. They live a double life that they use to cover-up their illegal smuggling ways. They are professional and know how to blend in to the regular routine world. The experienced ones move the drugs and do all of their work during daylight hours. The new, inexperienced dealers are the ones moving at night. The experienced dealers are not out flashing their money and luxury vehicles; they blend in. It is the new, inexperienced ones who are out flashing their cars, jewelry, and cash. These are the easy targets, and they are the ones who lead to the bigger fish. Even the churro lady outside of the "super" or grocery store is selling cocaine out of her churro cart. Have you ever seen a churro lady roll out in an Escalade?

The undercover world is an interesting one. Having worked undercover for so many years, I know the importance of blending in. The hot and sexy Angelina Jolie-type whose hair and makeup looks perfect while sliding down the side of building does not exist. Sorry to break your undercover dreams. We smell, we watch our surroundings, we drive the cars that criminals drive, and we wear the clothes they wear. You don't get to shower, or worry about your hair and makeup, until you are done being on post. But again, this is old-school undercover. Undercover looks a lot different today. There is also extreme undercover—being an informant, also known as a rat, or even an undercover participant. Meaning, you are one of the criminals, just undercover. You are killing, dealing, smuggling, and completely immersed in the culture. These brave souls risk their lives for everything. In fact, agents get murdered, decapitated, and their heads placed on stakes for display. This world is not an exciting one—it is a dark and heinous one. But what brings me solace is the fact that someone has to do this work.

Also, once you have killed, and once you've accepted the fact you have taken a life, it becomes easier to do it again. It is either kill or be killed. This is true in government work, and obviously in the military. There are even those who are better at ending lives than others. The government has highly trained, highly sought-after assassins. They are paid handsomely, and that is their job: to wipe out whomever they are paid to wipe out. You grow thick skin, and you start seeing life in a different light. Life is precious and valuable. I squeeze every single drop out of life that I possibly can. There are also some who see the afterlife as more valuable than the world we live in.

Terrorists are a whole different breed. Just like human traffickers and drug dealers, they enjoy the lifestyle. All are ready and willing to die. But terrorists, in my opinion, are the most ready to end their lives because they believe they have a higher purpose. The definition of a terrorist is someone with political motives who unlawfully utilizes violence against civilians. There are actually six different types of terrorists: the new, the state, the dissident, the religious, the ideological, and the international. Terrorists use different tactics to terrorize, such as hijackings, kidnappings, bombings, assassinations, armed assaults, and barricade-hostage incidents. The objectives of a terrorist are simple: to unleash great fear on their target with an intent to having a lasting emotional impact.

Terrorists are getting younger and younger. Terrorists are also not all foreign. There are many qualities and characteristics, but they are usually the same across the board with terrorists, gang members, murderers, killers, drug dealers, hackers, and everybody else under the sun who causes havoc on national security. Most of the scum of the earth are usually violent in nature, coming from alcoholic, drug abusing, or violent families, having a deep faith, and most often being sexually passive, shy, or timid. Most of them have few or poor social skills, an inability to form deep emotional connections, are emotionally unavailable, have a deep longing for acceptance, and most likely have extremely low self-worth. Wanting economic aid and assistance for their families is also a strong motivating factor. Once you've drunk the terrorist Kool-Aid, it is hard to put down.

Suicide bombings are not considered suicide, which comes with mental disturbance. Suicide bombers are considered holy warriors, and have the highest level of respect from their peers. They also do not consider themselves murderers. They are all fueled by the desire for honor and respect. In my opinion, it always goes back to the childhood experiences, stories, and ultimately, how we interpreted what happened to us. As long as conflicts exist, terrorists will continue to exist as well.

CHAPTER 18

THE CAPITAL

At one point in my career, I was sent to work in Washington D.C. for a month. This was the first time I was exposed to such an array of federal buildings in one place. Most of my investigations took place in all different types of buildings, including the Pentagon. Working inside the Pentagon was very cool. The building itself is extremely neat. It is a massive labyrinth on the inside that is not supposed to make any sense. I happened to be there during September 11, the anniversary of the attacks on the Pentagon and the World Trade Center, and was invited to the remembrance event taking place there. Having a plane crash into our country's defense building was insane. You can tell where the plane crashed into the Pentagon because that section was rebuilt. It was a sight to see. The most interesting thing about the Pentagon is that it is a field of energy. The Pentagon eats the energy from your devices. You have to turn off your cell phones because the building sucks up all the energy. I thought it was a myth, but it is true.

One does not just casually waltz into any government building. Security is heavy, armed, and everywhere. It is by no means easy to infiltrate a government building. Let this sink in for a minute. Entering a government building is not easy at all, unless you are let in. Once when entering a federal building, and I gave my

ID to one of front guards, they did not give me my ID back. I entered the building, conducted my investigation, and came back out. When I came out and asked the guard for my ID back, he said he had given it to me. He had by no means given me my ID. With his word against mine, the blame was put on me. With all the cameras at this building, I requested for the footage to be reviewed. For them to review the footage, I had to get the permission of a federal judge. To do that, I would have to hire a federal attorney to file a motion to have the video at the building reviewed. One thing I learned quickly is that government agencies are free standing, meaning, they do their work and every other agency stands alone. Somebody had to be blamed for the "loss" of my ID, and it wasn't the guard—it was me. I received a violation for "losing government property." I was sent home, fined, docked pay, and suspended from work for two weeks. The punishments for those who break the rules in government work are not pretty; at least that is the case for those who don't hold a super high position. The big shots in the government can get away with more. The ID incident left a sour taste in my mouth. I do exceptional work, my investigations are crisp and flawless, and my reports are impeccable. Yet, being an outstanding investigator does not make you untouchable.

I witnessed a lot of rule-breaking and a lot of slaps on the wrist from the higher-ups, but my slap on the wrist felt like a punch in the gut. Working for the government comes at a cost. If you get in trouble, you can get fired, fined, suspended, demoted or—even worse—end up in federal prison. Losing credentials and IDs are not something you want to happen. If you lose a badge, you get fined close to $2,000. We have to secure our government property completely, just as we do our cases, our laptops, and all of our files, which are all full of top-secret information.

I learned a lot from my experience in DC. Within the government elite, everyone knows each other; they all hang out and party, and are part of a clique with government power. The parties are super fancy, and the attitudes and noses are high. I can only imagine how trying to fit in is a difficult feat. Being liked, accepted, and welcomed is what everyone hopes for.

One thing is for sure, the higher up you are in government, the more rules you can break and the more untouchable you become. Some of the things that have become public about breaching oaths would land an investigator like myself a first-class ticket to federal prison. How can someone so high up in the government get away with so much, and when someone like me loses an ID, I get suspended, fined, and sent home? I've witnessed many examples of this type of double standard. People have been punished for things such as stealing a case of toilet paper from a government building with cameras everywhere (not a smart thing to do). But then people in high positions are having sex in the mailrooms with secretaries, getting caught with drugs, prostitutes, and even caught looking at porn on government-issued computers. This is a huge violation, as browsing any nefarious website becomes a national security breach, as it is a way for hackers to gain access to government systems. Watching porn on government-issued computers while on government property just goes to show how addicted some of these officials are. They do it knowing that it's a huge security violation. The amount of corruption involved in the government is staggering. The name of the game is to get away with it by any means possible.

A lot of rule-breaking and corruption goes on in the military too. In fact, most of the head-turning stories happen within the military. I believe the military has a broken system where many soldiers suffering from post-traumatic stress disorder do not receive proper mental health treatment. Many of the investigations that I conducted within military involved young kids simply doing dumb things, while other high-level personnel were just not thinking through their decisions.

Being a woman in a male-dominant field can be like torture. Most of the men in power undress you with their eyes, hit on you, and get upset when you don't reciprocate. A lot of women keep their heads down and their mouths shut. A lot of men will say vulgar things around women—some extremely sexual in nature—and will try anything to get in your pants. It is up to the women to take a strong stand. When I started working for the government, I told myself I would never engage in any behavior other than being professional with my colleagues. I once got my workload cut in half because I refused to ride in a helicopter with a supervisor. The way he asked, while looking me up and down, made me sick to my stomach, "Do you want to ride my chopper?" I looked around the room and saw the two female admins look down, avoiding eye contact with me. When I said, "No!" I saw how wide the other male agents' eyes became. This was an indication of how this supervisor had been chewing people out. Because I refused his advances, he cut my workload in half . . . meaning that I would only get half pay. When I asked why he did this, he gave me the go-to, "We are having IT issues" explanation. There are a lot of narcissistic, chauvinistic, misogynist, sex-addicted males working in government. But this I am sure you already know.

Today's world is a digital one, and our phones listen to us, literally. People make it easy for their lives to be infiltrated by posting their every move, favorite food place, and hang out spot online. We are so connected to our devices that most investigations can be done by simply hacking into phones. Phones can be pinged and located as long as they are on and working. This is why drug dealers, criminals, terrorists, and true criminal minds use burner phones that they regularly throw out and replace. Because we are so connected, old-school surveillance like I experienced is unnecessary, and IT experience is highly valued these days.

Aliens exist. If they didn't, why would the Pentagon spend sixty years funding UFO research? This is not something new. If you had any doubts about the existence of life in space, well, here is your answer—*it does exist.* The Defense Department budget is $600 billion, and $22 million was used for the Advanced Aerospace Threat Identification Program. This program investigated unidentified flying objects. Who or what do you think is flying these UFOs? While government officials have never explicitly said aliens exist, or that they have visited Earth, this is not top-secret knowledge and it became public information in April of 2020. We are not alone on this Earth.

There is a lot of video footage of military encounters with UFOs. One incident that occurred off the coast of San Diego in 2004 involved two A-18F fighter jets chasing a UFO. This is no longer a secret—the Pentagon's UFO Unit have made some findings public. The Navy released three ominous UFO videos. There is even an Unidentified Aerial Phenomenon Task Force. Make no mistake, materials—pieces of the UFOs that had crashed to Earth—are in the possession of the government. Even though Senator Reid backtracked on his original comment that the U.S. government had been hiding important information about UFOs for many years, and the Pentagon says it has dismantled its once-covert program, the existence of UFOs does not remain in question anymore.

Here we humans are on Earth not knowing how to get along with each other, yet there exists an entire world of unearthly creatures with immense technology and capabilities. I can only imagine what these creatures think of us as they witness humans fighting with each other like idiots. In my opinion, they are better off wherever they come from.

CHAPTER 19

EQUILIBRIA

At the end of 2013, I parted ways and left the government world to do something totally different. The government contract world is a cyclical one, with many ups and downs. I was also sick of the bullshit. When things happen, you are either blamed, fired, furloughed, or kept in the dark about your future. Sometimes being fired seems like a better solution than sticking around and not having any work to do. By this time, many government contract agencies had gone belly up or crashed and burned. I needed a break—something different, exciting, interesting, and non-government affiliated. I left the government world for two years, and during this time I began to explore diversity of thought and self-awareness.

In January of 2014, I was invited to attend a board meeting for Cherish Our Children International (COCI), a non-profit I had been involved with since 2009. I had been the team leader for their fundraising efforts. With a great team and Gabrielle by my side, we managed to raise over $120,000 that year. COCI and all of its programs, including "No More Victims," have been an important part of my life. At the meeting, I met a man named Lewis Senior, who was also in attendance. Lewis is the co-founder and CEO of Equilibria, a company that specializes in diversity of thought, self-awareness,

personal, professional, and organizational performance by identi-
fying individualistic personality traits and tendencies. Lewis spoke
about what he had created with Equilibria, his vision, and what he
intended to accomplish with the E-Colors program. He explained
that there are a total of twelve E-Color combinations. I learned that
I am a Yellow/Red—a "doing socializer." I love to talk, be around
people, laugh, have a good time, and get things done. I sometimes
get things done without reading all the directions or instructions,
therefore completing a task quickly . . . but most likely incorrectly. I
don't do well with details, can go off on tangents, and have a thousand thoughts going through my brain at once.

Lewis is a fun, loving, and exciting man. He is British but speaks
fluent Spanish. This makes him even more captivating. He is
wonderful with words and has an intriguing story about a near-
death experience. Lewis had so much conviction, passion, and love
for his E-Colors concept that whatever he was up to, I wanted to
be a part of it. I introduced myself to Lewis, telling him, "I want to
be a part of what you are doing."

Two months later I was off and running with Equilibria, traveling all
over the U.S. with Dr. Rosalinda Mercado, a fellow Yellow/Red.
I worked as an education communication coach with E-Colors
in Education, which was a program that familiarized school-aged
children with the different personality types. I got to visit many
schools and meet some incredible students who were extremely
versed in E-Colors. I wished I would have had this knowledge as
a child; I would have saved my mother a lot of therapy sessions
and a lot of broken lamps. I was an angry kid with a lot of trauma.
Through my journey working with Equilibria, I learned a great deal
about myself, my tendencies, my personality traits, and I learned
how to communicate much more effectively with others. There are

specific ways to communicate with people in a way that is superior, and doing so will get you results. Lack of communication is a huge problem in schools, hospitals, organizations, and the government. E-Colors gives you access to efficient communication tools in order to get tasks done, make requests of people, and allow leaders to lead intentionally. My experience working with Equilibria was grand, amazing, and eye-opening. It was fun, exciting, and completely rewarding. At one of our sessions, I had a breakdown with the realization that, for many years, I carried a huge burden on my back about my adolescent trauma. E-Colors allowed me to release the trauma that was still lingering. Lewis Senior runs his company with his gorgeous, statuesque daughter Laura, a Red/Yellow, and his handsome, calm, loving son David, a Blue/Yellow (Relating Socializer). I had the privilege of working with all three of them, and it was very rewarding. After a two-year break, and with my newfound knowledge, I returned to work for the government.

I decided to return to the government and do what I do best—interrogate. But this time, I was going to do it on my own watch, with my own company. I started my own investigative firm. I called it Adevar Investigative Group. "Adevar" means "truth" in Romanian. All of the contracts I serviced were federal. I signed a contract to have a license to utilize Eye Detect, the new technology that is replacing the outdated polygraph. It takes sixty thousand measurements of your retina to detect dilation, which indicates deception. Being the CEO of my own company was extremely rewarding. As a leader, I grew and learned so much. Utilizing my experience in the field, my knowledge of E-Colors, and my own self-development really helped my business succeed. Being a government contractor allows you to work for numerous government agencies with numerous contracts and get exposed to many fields.

CHAPTER 20

GOD'S GIFTS

In 2014, I qualified for a race in San Francisco called "Escape from
Alcatraz." For this race, you're first taken out on a ferry with all
the competitors from the coast of the San Francisco Bay to Alcatraz. A whistle is blown, and you jump off the boat and swim for
your life to shore. This was by far one of the most amazing and terrifying experiences of my life. Not even having ten guns pointed
at my head was as terrifying as this experience. I always explain to
people that not only is the water of San Francisco Bay cold as hell
(about 45°F), but it is also treacherous and full of sharks. You must
have already met a qualifying swim time to survive this swim. I
came a long way with my swimming, from being the last one out
of the water in my first triathlon to qualifying for one of the hardest swims in the world. I always explain to people: Imagine trying
to swim straight while you're inside a rotating washing machine.
This is exactly what it's like swimming in San Francisco Bay. This
race was the last triathlon I would take part in before finishing my
triathlon hobby, and I went out with a bang. I had returned to
triathlon racing after completely destroying my ankle in 2011. This
was a bucket-list triathlon for me, and I wasn't going to miss the
opportunity to experience it. The difficult, mountainous bike ride,
the picturesque run along the gorgeous shoreline of San Francisco

Beach with the Golden Gate Bridge as the backdrop were like a dream.

Dr. Beckman had told me that trail running would strengthen my newly repaired ankle. I decided to try it out, and was quickly hooked. The uneven terrain of trail running along with being in a different natural environment brought me an entirely new perspective on racing. Being in nature and exploring the trails was both exhilarating and cathartic. All my triathlon friends were also obsessed with trail running; many had done ultra-marathons, 50-milers, and even 100-mile runs. I know . . . we're crazy people, but I loved it. It was like being free to roam, and no swimming or biking was required.

In March of 2014, I had been training for my first fitness competition, a body-building competition where you strut your stuff in a teeny-tiny bikini while being judged. Being part of a fitness competition had also been an item on my bucket list. Ray and I went to the gorgeous Hill Country for our anniversary and had a whole weekend of activities planned. Sadly, it rained all weekend, so the two of us were left with only each other for entertainment. That night we conceived our intelligent, witty, extraordinary Belén. My pregnancy meant that I could not compete in my fitness competition. Ray and I were scared, but feeling excited and blessed at the same time. Being pregnant did not slow me down one bit. In fact, I embraced it and took this unborn baby with me to run two half marathons. I was four months pregnant, and with my friends Alida and Ingrid we went to Grand Teton and Yellowstone National Parks. It was an extraordinary trip. We had the greatest time, the best conversations, the best food, and the most gorgeous scenery to explore. I ran two trail half-marathons at a high elevation while pregnant with Belén. It sounds crazy, but it was freaking amazing! Two weeks later I was back to working for the government doing national security cases.

Our daughter was born in December of 2015, and our lives were changed forever. Belén was born with her eyes wide open, ready to take on the world. This little girl came with a double dose of my defiant, inquisitive, explorative DNA. She is highly intelligent; a genius little girl who will grow up to move mountains. This curly-haired blessing was truly a gift from God to us. She brought so much joy to our lives, and our strong partnership now had a wide-eyed little face observing our every move. Becoming a parent is truly a gift. You are now responsible for keeping this tiny fragile human alive and kicking. They say that becoming a parent changes you, and it certainly does. It makes you more accountable for your actions and words. It is true—no one knows the real meaning of love until they look into the eyes of their child. I embraced motherhood, and loved it. I now had a little partner in crime to take everywhere with me. Ray and I vowed that our lives would not change with the addition of our new child, and that we would still live a life of excitement, adventure, and joy. Our children would be additions to this wonderful life we had created.

So, the fun began. I took Belén to Mexico, San Francisco, and Florida before she even turned one. I wanted to start her adventures off young, so she grew up loving adventure, travel, and experiencing life to the fullest. After Belén turned one, we planned for a second child. Despite having only half of my cervix, I never had a problem getting pregnant. In fact, I was able to have my two babies naturally, thanks to the scar tissue that had grown over my cervix—another blessing in disguise. We found out that I was pregnant in January of 2016. We planned on surprising our family with the news of a second baby on Valentine's Day. But while I was on a job at NASA, I felt a horrible pain in my uterus. I was walking through the NASA campus when I began to bleed. I miscarried our second child.

Miscarriages are more common than I had previously thought. The loss of a child is a hard one. I was torn to pieces, sad, and hurt. Watching your baby dissolve out of you is a horrible experience. Wanting a child so badly and then losing it in an instant is hard to accept. This event was hard on me. I had aborted two pregnancies in my life, and now I had lost a child that I wanted. I saw it as something of a punishment, and I hurt deeply. I was depressed, inconsolable, and felt deep regret for the babies I had aborted. In my pain of losing this child, I asked God for forgiveness. I was so distraught that I went to a miscarriage therapy group to try to deal with the loss. The biggest pain for a mother is losing a child. I felt shame and embarrassment that I had ended two prior pregnancies. I seriously believed that this was God's way of punishing me for destroying two other blessings that he had sent to me before. Ray was also hurt and saddened, but he was supportive of me. I stayed up late reading about unborn babies going to heaven. I do believe in the afterlife, and I do believe our loved ones are always around us and watching. I also believe that unborn babies' souls go to heaven and are taken care of by our loved ones who have passed. I like to believe that when it's my time to go, I will see my three unborn babies in heaven. It may sound crazy to some, but this is what I believe.

Therapy is powerful. I have the utmost respect for mental health professionals because they work to make a huge difference in the lives of so many people. Four months after my miscarriage, we tried again, and were gifted with our rainbow baby, Zion. Having a baby at thirty-seven is considered high-risk, and I was treated as such. When I was pregnant with Zion, I was part of a boxing club. I didn't box with other people, but I trained with punching bags and jump ropes. I had always been super active, athletic, and in shape. I was diagnosed with placenta previa, which is when the placenta covers the opening of the cervix. This condition can cause the mother to bleed out and die. As a result, I was put on bed rest for the rest of the pregnancy, which meant that I could not be out there boxing, or working national security cases. Luckily for me, the previa resolved before Zion was born.

I have made some incredible friends in my life, and I couldn't write a chapter on God's gifts without mentioning them. I have surrounded myself with wonderful people who commiserate in my sorrows and celebrate in my successes. I met green-eyed, curly-haired, doll-looking Jenny at a CrossFit gym. We instantly became friends and grew a special bond. Jenny is an officer in the Navy and the mother of three beautiful daughters. She has been one of my best friends and one of the most dependable human beings I have ever known. She would always come through when I needed her. The two of us have a lot in common. We love to party, have a good time, and occasionally go off on tangents. Our talks can be like five conversations in one. She has been by my side in many dark times. Even though she is off living on the other side of the country, we keep in contact regularly, and it is as if she never left.

Natalie, I met through Chris. Chris went to college with Ray at Houston Baptist University, and the two were friends. I met Natalie at my engagement party. She is an adorable, loving, doll-like woman. She has the biggest heart, and is like a little sister to me. She is eight years younger than I am, but we have so much fun together. We also have a lot in common, and have built a gorgeous friendship. We share a very special bond: we have both have felt deep loss in our lives, and our babies are only one month apart in age. We got to share our pregnancies together, and I always joke that my son Zion will marry her daughter Mackenzie. She has been such a wonderful friend to me. She has cried when I cried, laughed when I laughed, and celebrated when I celebrated. I love you ladies.

CHAPTER 21

TRAGEDY STRIKES AGAIN

On November 26, 2017, two days before my thirty-seventh birthday, I received the most horrible call. Bill, Gabrielle's husband, called me, and with a very calm voice, informed me that my friend Devon Wade had been murdered. I screamed and cried with anguish. Devon Wade was a star, a ray of light—a brilliant, simply amazing soul. He had experienced a traumatic childhood. He was a child of incarcerated parents, and was involved in COCI's program "No More Victims." Devon was an incredible scholar who had won many awards, along with a scholarship to LSU. He had been studying to defend his dissertation for his PhD at Columbia University. I met Devon in 2009 when he was a young graduating high school senior. He had so much love and light in his eyes. He was out to create greatness in the world.

Over the years, I had trained many people on how to swim for triathlons, and would often invite people to come to our residential twenty-five meter community pool. Devon came over in the August prior to his death, and we worked on his swimming. He was ready to compete in his first triathlon and wanted some tips on his swimming technique. We had an amazing time, talking about books, life, traveling, and everything under the sun. Devon said we could talk forever, but we had been in the pool so long his fingers were getting wrinkly. The next month, in September, Ray and I had a party in which Devon and his boyfriend Mario attended. We all had so much fun. Devon was always full of life, and was a pure pleasure to be around. I talked to Mario, who was an engineer, and the two of them seemed very happy. Never in a million years did I ever think that Mario would murder Devon. I had talked to many murderers throughout my career. I later told Ray that we had a murderer in our home.

Devon and Mario had a dispute. Mario left the home and returned with a gun. When he came back to Devon's house, the two had another dispute and Mario shot Devon killing him instantly. Mario later turned himself in to the authorities. The death of Devon felt like the world stopped turning. Devon was an angel on Earth. He was the type of person God puts on this Earth to make a difference in the lives of many. And the same way that God put him on this Earth, he also took him away.

Devon had a tough childhood, but turned his life around with the love and support of Ms. Marilyn Gambrell, the founder and creator of the No More Victims (NMV) program. NMV is a program for kids of incarcerated parents; a support system for children to be able to graduate high school and pursue higher education. Kids of incarcerated parents usually end up in jail as well, but Ms. Gambrell's program was changing the path for many of these kids.

Mario was charged with the murder of Devon. While we were mourning the loss of a pillar and trying to wrap our minds around this tragedy, Mario was released on a $100,000 bond. The community outpouring of love for Devon was overwhelming. Family, friends, teachers, and colleagues all came together to celebrate Devon's life. His funeral was incredible, and so many people attended that the huge cathedral was packed to the brim. Super pregnant and completely crushed, I sat at the back of the church crying uncontrollably. I am good at keeping a straight face during interrogations and showing no emotion—I have perfected that—but when something like this happens so close to home, I couldn't help but break down. I sat as far back as I could, as I do not like seeing dead bodies, especially of those I love. I have seen plenty of dead bodies, but the thought of putting someone on display that looks nothing like their true self does not sit well with me. I want to remember my loved ones happy, full of life, and smiling . . . not lying in a box, lifeless and gone.

A month after Devon was buried, Mario hanged himself, taking his own life. When I found out about this, I was saddened—saddened that there had once been so much love between them, and Mario's way out of the ordeal was to take his own life. I hurt for both mothers, since they both had sons who were no longer on this Earth. I prayed for both of their souls because I know how it is to be in a suicidal frame of mind. It means that the only solution is to simply cease to exist. Mario must have felt that the pain in his heart was too much to bear, too much to deal with. I wondered for many nights about the thoughts that went through Mario's mind. But both are gone now, and tragedy is part of life.

In February of 2018, I gave birth to my little boy, Zion, who made quite an entrance. After two epidurals and the pain of childbirth, I almost died trying to give birth to this little miracle. When you are induced and the epidural does not work, your contraction pain is ten times more than giving birth naturally. I pushed and pushed for an hour, and Zion was not coming out. I was bleeding and could feel myself losing strength, and I was barely grasping to my consciousness. Finally, when his head came out, the umbilical cord was wrapped around his neck. As I pushed, the cord kept pulling Zion back into my womb. Ray was so traumatized by the birth he made an appointment to get a vasectomy as soon as possible.

As the doctor checked Ray over, he looked at him and said, "I think you only have one kidney." After an ultrasound, we found out that Ray had indeed been born with only one kidney. This was a huge surprise, since Ray had been an extremely healthy athlete his entire life. Not even his mother had been made aware that he only had one kidney. His one kidney was large and healthy, but he was no longer allowed to play any contact sports. I told Ray that not knowing may have been a blessing, because his childhood would have been spent indoors, not playing baseball. Ray played baseball his entire life. He was coached by his father and was part of a select travel team. Ray even played baseball at Houston Baptist University. Now he takes care of the one kidney as much he can.

Eight months later, tragedy struck again. Melbin Batista, my sister-in-law's husband and the best man at our wedding, died tragically in a car accident. Melbin was driving home after work in the early hours of the morning after having worked a long night shift. He lost control of his vehicle on a road that he had traveled regularly. His car struck a tree, and he died instantly. Melbin left behind his wife and three kids. When I heard the news that he had passed, it was another shock and hit to the heart. Melbin was a loving and gentle man who always wanted to help others. He was here one day and gone the next. Life is precious and also fragile. It can be taken away very quickly. The road on which Melbin died was one that many others had also died in the same manner, crashing into the same tree. The most painful sound I have ever heard was the sound of his three children crying when their mother told them their father was gone. I remember this day vividly, as we were all sitting in our living room. When Ray's sister Maggie told all three kids their father had passed, they screamed and cried uncontrollably, and all we could do was hold them tight.

CHAPTER 22

CRASH AND BURN

Extreme exhaustion had set in. I was a walking zombie. I could not fall asleep or stay asleep for long. I was exhausted in the mornings and wide awake at night. I had body aches, digestive issues, and my emotions were all over the map. I was irritable, my hair was falling out, and my eyes hurt. It was time to make a drastic change. I no longer resembled a person who I wanted to be. Being a government contractor running my own company was a lot of work, which eventually led to massive burn out.

My dear friend Gabrielle invited me to complete the Landmark curriculum and enroll in the advanced course in June 2019. For eight years I had resisted the advanced course, but I knew I deserved it. The Advanced course is the second course of the curriculum, during which you use your newfound tools to create a future of your own design. It was time to take back control of my own life. I took an entire month off work to recollect and to really begin to work on myself. It was time for a restoration. I took an honest look at myself and was ready to make a swift change.

I complained about my weight, and I swore to myself that I was doing everything I could possibly do to lose it. I was obsessed with earning those high-paying checks for four days of work. The problem was that the job was actually fourteen days of work crammed into four. I was doing ten investigations a day for four straight days. My motive was to make as much money as possible in as little time as possible. I became money-hungry, and earning a lot of money in four days became an addiction. I had placed so much importance on my self-worth being determined by the money I was bringing in. I quickly learned that money did not mean anything. I had made this type of crazy money before doing undercover work, so one would have thought that I would have learned this lesson early. But as a young woman, getting to see the world, hiding in the shadows, and cashing in on a huge paycheck became an addiction.

I went to six doctors to try to find out what was happening to me. I went through various tests and diagnostic procedures in hopes of obtaining some answers. Why was I feeling so miserable? They all said the same thing: "You are overweight." I was overweight and I did need to lose some. I was in a body that I did not recognize. I had always been extremely fit and athletic. When one doctor wanted to put me on metformin, that was the final straw. I had been working with a wonderful nutritionist, Lindsey, who was one of the most beautiful women I had ever seen. She had the type of calm that one could only dream of. With porcelain skin and long wispy hair, she was a vision of pure, vibrant health. She was the kind of woman who, when she walked into a room, angel harps would play in the background. Lindsey was as baffled as I was, but we both knew Western doctors were going to be a dead end. She insisted I take a DUTCH test, which tests hormone levels at different times of the day. This test uncovered the real tragedy that was going on inside my body. My hormones were so out of whack that she could not believe I was even functioning. I was a real-life walking zombie. I felt dead inside, but now it had caught up with me.

I gave up on Western medicine and refused the metformin prescription. I searched the web for a new solution, an alternative medicine, and came across Dr. Julia Ward's office for Balanced Body Functional Medicine. I quickly called her and made an appointment. Dr. Ward is a strong woman with beautiful long blonde hair. Not only is she beautiful, but she is also a competitive fitness champion. Dr. Ward has an incredible body. She became my savior. She and her team brought me back to life. After many blood tests and looking over my Dutch test, she uttered, "You have stage four adrenal fatigue." Adrenal fatigue is not something that Western doctors ever talk about, or even like to discuss at all. From my understanding, it is not even something that they believe in. Dr. Ward, an MD, was different. She had spent her life dealing with women like me—women who were going about their lives running purely on fumes. How in the hell was I functioning, working national security, in zombie mode? With meticulous supplementation, hormone revamping, a change in eating, sleeping, and an overhaul of my stress levels, it did not take long for me to gain my life back. I always told her that I came in feeling like a zombie and walked out feeling like a million bucks. I became her star patient. The local newspaper even did a story on my recovery because it was a complete 180°.

I had regained my health, but the weight was not coming off fast enough. It was now January of 2020, and I had decided I was going to compete in a fitness competition. This had been a dream of mine for over five years. The last time I was in the process of competing, a night of anniversary passion left me pregnant with my daughter, Belén. I hired a trainer, Shannon, at a local gym. I wanted to hire the trainer that was in the best shape ever, and Shannon's body was a work of art. To me, if the trainer is taking care of their own body first, then they can tell me how to take care of mine. I had worked with many trainers in the past and had already been lifting for many years. But when Shannon walked into a room, guys and girls were falling off the stair-masters and treadmills. Not only was she stunning, but when she turned to the side, her booty was a masterpiece. I wanted a body like hers and was willing to put in the work. Shannon and I began working together, and I was having good results when the COVID-19 pandemic hit. Now gyms were closed, and everyone was on lockdown.

I spent hours online looking for at-home workouts and fasting regimens and came across a gentleman named Cole Robinson. His videos were offensive, crude, and insulting, but I was hooked. He talked about prolonged fasting and how when you fast, your body feasts on its own body fat. I watched about five of his videos, and decided to contact him and hire him as my fasting coach. Cole rubs many people the wrong way due to his insulting, "in-your-face approach," an approach that did not seem to bother me. His results were incredible, and I wanted them. I worked with Cole, and by September of 2020, had lost more than fifty pounds. I looked like a whole different person. My health and longevity were back. I began living a fasting-focused lifestyle. I quickly gained recognition on social media, since Cole posted my before and after pictures. I began getting flooded with countless messages from women wanting to lose weight.

During my weight loss journey, I had seen the incredible transformation of a gorgeous blonde named Monika. I reached out to her on social media for advice. Monika and I have never met in person, but we became each other's accountability partners and close friends. We started a women's mindful-eating and fasting group with the intent to help women all over the world. Our group currently has over four thousand women all with the same goal—to lose weight and be hot. Monika and I have shared our ups and downs with weight loss, binge eating, and learning how to deal with food addictions. Not only did we both lose a combined weight of over one hundred thirty pounds and started a successful fasting group called The Real Snake Diet for Women, Fasting & Mindful Eating, but soon, Monika and I will be gracing the fitness competition stage.

CHAPTER 23

GROWTH

I had just completed a three-day training session where I had the opportunity to understand the enemy at a much deeper level. My husband, Ray, had a chance to read this book in its early stages. His insecurities ran wild and his emotions even higher. This book triggered him immensely. Ray finally told me the truth: his father had been in the drug selling business, selling millions of dollars in drugs. My jaw dropped to the floor, and I felt like I must have died momentarily. My husband had kept this secret from me for all ten years of our relationship. Out of fear of losing me, he never told me this before we got married. And rightfully so—I would not have married him. I have enough self-development and self-awareness to know it took him so much courage and strength to reveal this secret. I quickly switched from being an astonished, pissed-off wife to being a listening interrogator in the blink of an eye.

As I processed this news, it was clear that this secret would have a detrimental impact on my life. I had held a top-secret clearance for fifteen years. I had been working for the government in many different capacities, always being exposed to top-secret information. I am personally investigated every five years as a process to renew my top-secret clearance. I am considered one of the best interrogators in the world, and the man that I married, the family

I married into, had been involved with the mexican cartel. We are talking about millions of dollars in drugs, not just a few ounces here and there. In fact, Ray disclosed that his uncle had been murdered transporting a million dollars worth of cocaine up the East Coast.

As my entire life flashed before my eyes when he shared this information, I kept my cool. But inside, the anger began to bubble. I had been deceived, betrayed, and lied to. I married into a family that I thought was loving and pure. They were far from that. His family did not think about the impact and severity this secret would have on my career, my children, and my life. It was hard to wrap my mind around all of this—that this was my reality—but in this moment, my husband had been the most authentic he had ever been with me. In this moment, we had been the closest we had ever been. As twisted as it sounds, it was true. He told me he felt free.

How is it possible that I had been sleeping next to this man who had been holding this secret for a decade? How painful it must have been for him to keep this secret from me. I never liked his father. In fact, I never got along with him. There was always something off about him; he just never sat well with me, ever. That should have been my first indication that something was different. Even on my wedding day, I questioned the marriage. I told Gabrielle that I was afraid to marry Ray for fear that he was just like his father. Gabrielle calmed me down, and I went through with the marriage. Everyone told me that it was normal to have cold feet and be nervous. But I know now that my gut instinct was right on target. How could I be an expert in my field and not know this about my own family? Ray's father spent most of our marriage living abroad.

Ray had made a vow and broke it before I even walked down the aisle. With pain in my heart and anger in my mind, I told my husband that I had to report this information. There was no doubt in my mind that I had to inform the Security Department about this. I would not be able to live with myself, and I refused to live in fear. This situation is not something you take lightly when you spend hours on end listening to live drug deals going down, or people killing and being killed.

My entire career was on the line. I felt my life was over. I told Ray that I was going to report it, and he agreed with me. It was the right thing to do. What crossed my mind was that one day I would have to tell this story to our children, and it would be their biggest lesson in integrity. I am a person of utmost integrity, and I live a life fully self-expressed. I believe you are only as good as your word. I called my supervisor and told her the new piece of information I had learned. At this point, Ray and I had decided to separate because this was not something that you could just slide to the side. I wished he had told me he had slept with the Starbucks barista, or anything but this, but that was not the case.

My supervisor's jaw must have hit the ground too, because there had been silence for what seemed like an eternity. When she finally spoke, she did not know what to say. She said the information needed to be moved up the chain. In other words, this situation was above her pay scale. The head of security was also made aware, and I shared the news with her on the phone. At this point, I had told the story about five times, so I had really perfected the story line. She was just as surprised, if not more, than my supervisor. Her words were that she could not guarantee anything, and that I needed to write a full statement of the entire conversation. At this point, the separation date had to be added to this statement. It wasn't even a question of if I planned on staying in the marriage. The head of security said she had to pass this information on to the director of security. The director of security then had to pass it up to the "client," that being the Pentagon.

Now that the fate of my entire career was in the government's hands, tears began streaming down my face. All the time, sweat, tears, and blood I had given to the government lay in their hands. They were going to make the decision whether to keep me or blacklist me. The thought of having your entire career taken away from you by the decision of some bigshot had to be the darkest moment of my life. Everything I had worked for could be taken away in a second. The government would terminate me without batting an eye. I would never work for the government again. But integrity means everything to me. Never in a million years did I ever imagine this was going to be the way I went out. If I was going to go out, it was definitely going to be with a bang—a story so unbelievable that perhaps one day I could laugh about it. I thought about my children who one day will read this book and know the truth.

In my darkest hour, I lay on my bedroom floor, curled up in a ball crying until I was cried out. How could this have happened to me? How was this even my life? The anger flowed through my veins. I was lost, broken, and felt used. But I knew that in the lowest moments of one's existence is where growth occurs. I called my friend, Gabrielle, an expert at talking me off the ledge. The last time I had been in this position, I had been holding a jug of gasoline, ready to set my ex's car on fire. Gabrielle was equipped and always prepared for these situations. She has been my angel on Earth for years. This time was no exception, because the phone call with her changed my entire perspective on the situation. Her words of comfort, love, and expertise once again de-escalated the hate, anger, and angst that had overpowered me.

Gabrielle listed to my insane rant, and she really heard me. She also told me that I would recreate myself, and I could create anything I wanted. This was my opportunity to build myself up again. This had happened before; it was not the first time I rebuilt myself. As I listened to her wonderful words of love, I stopped crying and picked up the pieces one by one. I described the feeling as that of being hit by a speeding train and realizing that I was still alive, peeling myself off the ground, and realizing I had survived. She said this was not the end and reminded me that God works in mysterious ways. And deep down inside, I knew that my parting ways with the government world had been near in any case. This might not have been the most graceful way of exiting, but it was one way. And what a freaking story to go with it.

This was yet another bump that God chose to put in my path to see how I would handle it. The younger Angelica would have set the house on fire and taken down everyone in sight. But this new, self-developed, self-aware Angelica was refined, awake, and good enough to continue. I chose integrity, I chose my children, and although at that moment it seemed like my life was over, I knew that it was just the beginning of a new era for me.

Ray's father had manipulated him throughout his entire life. Ray had been living in fear his whole life. I knew this situation was not Ray's fault and that he was an innocent bystander. When Ray met me, we did fall in love, and out of fear of losing me, he kept this secret from me. Ray may finally be free, but the scars are deep. Our love was deep and true for me, but our marriage would not survive this. The impact that this secret had on my life and life's work was deep. But I was strong enough to know that my children would grow up with the truth and be freed from their grandfather's hold. Ray had been, and may still be, entangled in his father's web at the cost of me losing my entire career.

Nevertheless, I took responsibility for my part in this ten-year lie. I can look at myself in the mirror and know that I showed up in this marriage like a grenade. I know that my reaction to certain events and conversations may have not been the most inviting. I had once been described as a firecracker, and now a grenade with my finger on the pin, ready to explode. I know that I did not give Ray the best space for him to be able to tell me the truth. I was not perfect in this relationship, and want to take responsibility for not having my reactions in check. As a young adult, I would break things, smash lamps, and allow anger to overpower my judgement. Relationships are a two-way street, and perhaps I never gave Ray the comfort of being able to tell me anything due to my crazy explosive reactions.

This book has had a major impact on my own family and husband. I have already made a difference with this book. I know I will recreate myself and rise from the ashes like a phoenix because I chose to see the beauty in my struggle. Growth occurs in your darkest hour. I know that I am stronger, and as the dust settles, I only want the very best for both Ray and I. This great love I experienced was real, but the damage was too deep to repair. I love Ray as the father of my children. I am continuing to build a strong relationship with him for the sake of our children, because we will always be in each other's lives. I want to show my children that even when the unthinkable occurs, you can persevere through it. Forgiveness is something I have learned the hard way. I have love and compassion for Ray, and I forgive him. Forgiving never means forgetting. I stand by my decision, because it is the biggest lesson in integrity I can teach my children, even if it meant the end of my marriage.

CHAPTER 24

THE FUTURE

I have found that self-care and self-love have a profound impact on my overall functionality. As I navigate through this tough time of my life, I know that I am not alone and that I will be okay. What doesn't kill you makes you stronger, that is for sure. Although my wounds have not all healed, they will with enough time. I chose to share the wisdom born from experience, because as I was finishing this book, my life completely unraveled. We waste so much of our lives wanting to be different, when in reality we are enough just the way we are. We allow the thoughts and opinions of others to dictate our own self-perception. We scroll for endless hours looking at what everyone else is doing, filling our minds with more and more insecurities about ourselves—who we should be, how we should look, what job we should be doing, how much money we should be making, who we should be with, where we should be vacationing, and so on and so forth. We tell ourselves that we are not enough when we actually are. We fear both the known and the unknown. Fear consumes our very being, leaving us with feelings of inadequacy. The actions that make the biggest differences—like meditation, petting a dog, hugging a loved one, watching a sunset, sitting in the sunlight, practicing intentional deep breathing, listening to music, or reading a book— do not require any money at all.

Self-care is the food for our soul. It fills our tanks with an energizing appreciation for the beauty this life brings.

The future may not be written, but I know it will be grand. Life doesn't happen to us, it happens for us. I am fully self-expressed and am raising my children to live a life full of joy and aliveness. I am teaching my kids that they are only as good as their word. Always do what you say you are going to do. I know that as a parent we want to protect our children from the horrors of the world—the heartache and the heartbreak. But the reality is that we can handle anything. Nothing is ever too much to handle. That is all a story we tell ourselves. You can never take the experience away. It is our reactions to the events that we live through that make a huge difference. It is our outlook on life that really makes the difference in how we perceive our world. The world is a gorgeous place, and there is beauty all around us. We are all living in the same world, but self-awareness and self-development can separate us from others and get us moving on a path of progress. Ask yourself what things from your past you are still holding on to that may be stalling you.

My children are my world. I wish for them to thrive, and know that they get to choose and create the life they want. They are limitless and unstoppable, and their souls were created out of great love. The future is whatever possibility I choose to create. I plan on traveling the world—not to investigate people or to follow criminals through the shadows—but to inspire people. I want to motivate people to be the absolute best versions of themselves. My hope is that sharing my story will inspire people to look into their hearts and minds and make amends with their past. My goal in life is to be alive, to feel everything: the good, the bad, and everything in between. I don't want to be happy—I want to be alive! I left my past in the past where it belongs, and no longer allow it to dictate my present.

I honored my struggle because I was able to face it and not avoid it. Believe it or not, there is beauty in struggle. Stop waiting for happiness to come to you. Instead, bring the happiness to yourself. The truth does set you free, but you must be willing to set the truth free. I chose to write about it. Allow yourself to feel, because life is about living and feeling alive. Life is short, and only you can choose how you will experience it.

FINALLY LETTING GO

I'd like to share with you some of the hard-won wisdom I've acquired from my experiences. The past no longer controls me. If you allow the past to control you, it comes into your present, which then shows up in your future. You become a prisoner of your past. We have all experienced trauma at different levels. I have experienced a great deal of trauma, which made me want to pick a job where I could make a difference in the lives of other people—a job where my questions could be answered, where I could be a free spirit, and where I could be exposed to the horrors of the world. But in that horror, I learned to appreciate the finest and most minute details of happiness in life. I've learned to appreciate every experience, good and bad, and learned from every single individual who has crossed my path. I have taken a piece of them and each experience with me. Instead of shoving my experience into a bag of despair, I chose to reveal and express it. I am far from perfect. I have experienced some of the most gut-wrenching and mind-fucking things—things that I would never wish upon anyone. But I choose to take my experiences and turn them into grace, love, happiness, and joy.

Our days on this Earth are numbered, and we get to choose how we will live them, with whom we will navigate this life, and how we will spend our time and effort. Do not allow your past experiences to define who you really are. The potential in all of us is massive, magnificent, and vast. Choose to touch, move, and inspire those around you. There is power in that.

Loneliness, despair, depression, and insecurity will never go away. Negativities will always rear their ugly heads, but I have learned that it is the way we respond and react that really makes the difference. Choosing to learn how to deal with the emotions that arise is more important than dealing with the actual event.

We are intelligent beings, the most complicated living organisms to have ever existed because of how magnificent our minds are. We allow our minds and thoughts to overpower us completely and turn us into people we don't even know. Letting go of the fear of judgement and really loving yourself with all of your imperfections is a graceful place to arrive. It takes time, practice, and consistency. It takes dedication, motivation, and intentionality.

We are human, and we bring a lot of pain from our past into our present. Let go of what makes you miserable, sad, insecure, and uneasy. It is not worth your time, the space it takes up in your mind, or the effort it requires. Life is beautiful in all of its forms. Take a look, and you will see. It all starts with a change in how you communicate with yourself.

You have immense potential, and have not even begun to tap into it. You are good enough. The only person telling you that you are not, is you. Have compassion for yourself. Perfection is the lowest standard because perfection is not real, it does not exist. We were created to be imperfect, mistake-driven, and beautifully, intricately, and meticulously complicated. You are extraordinary. I do not have to convince you of that, rather, it is you who must believe it. When you do, everything—and I mean everything—will fall into place. Those who put you down are feeling the exact same way.

I went from throwing lamps when angered to being able to just listen calmly. Learn to not make something mean something else, or make situations worse than they already are by your reaction. Assumption is the lowest form of knowledge. Be with people, hear what they are saying, even when they are screaming at the top of their lungs. Without noise, people will not be woken up. Something I learned from my life coach, Jen Lee, is that when people hurt you with their own insecurities and shortcomings, they are using a marshmallow gun. If you want to be like someone, get to know them, see what they are doing, and how their thought process functions. I guarantee you have more in common with them than you think.

I leave you with this: Your past is not thinking of you, why are you thinking of it?

Having let go of your past, try to find your purpose for the future. You don't have to find your "one purpose" in life—you can have more than one purpose! Have you ever heard of imposter syndrome? Imposter syndrome is alive and well. It's simply how we tell ourselves that we are not enough. It comes and goes, and it's always rearing its head. Even the most successful and powerful people on this Earth experience imposter syndrome all the time. Overachievers describe fear as stress, but when you boil it all down, it is fear. We live in fear of not being enough, not making enough, not having enough. Fear is what holds us back from living to our full potential. We learn fear at a very early age, and it sticks with us until the day we die. You can't hold fear in your hands. Fear is not a physical thing; it is a feeling that we manifest in our minds.

Fear is what stunts our growth and our mind, and takes up an overabundance of room in our own thoughts. Feelings of fear will always be there, but when you get to a place where you can acknowledge it and extinguish it, the conversation with yourself will shift. Growth will emerge.

What I have found to be extremely rewarding in my life's journey is to be of service to others. There is such fulfillment and joy in being of service and in helping others succeed. Celebrating the accomplishments of others has always been a great source of fuel for me. I enjoy seeing others thrive, grow, and win. Get out of your head, stop worrying about you, and serve others. Life is about giving something, not getting something. Find those people and things you love or that interest you, and serve. See how you thrive when you become of service to others. Surround yourself with people you want to emulate, and learn from their habits, their tendencies, their commitments. Surround yourself with people who love to serve others.

Dedicate yourself to being the author of your own story, because only you have the power to determine the course of your life. As you grow in your journey, you will realize how skilled you are, and more life purposes will arise. As you evolve, you will realize that we are the ones who dramatize our lives and make them more difficult than they appear to be. Strive to be better each day. One day we will all cease to exist, and we will no longer feel anything, so until that day, live your life, alive!

AFTERWORD

Angelica has always been a great friend to talk to and get advice from. What I appreciate from her, in addition to her candor, is her perspective. She doesn't tiptoe around topics, and is very direct, as you will know from reading this book, or if you've had the pleasure of engaging in conversation with her. This is something that was evident since the moment I met Angelica in 2001 in our dorm. We instantly bonded and our friendship has only strengthened since.

Angelica has always followed her passions and goals, which led her on the various journeys that she has captured in this book. Some of it through self-discovery, and some of it has been thrown at her. Without a doubt, Angelica has handled her ups and downs with integrity, and her intentions have always been pure. Her unique way of sharing stories from her life is what can keep you invested and reading.

She knew that the lessons she gained during her time of self-reflection were lessons that she wanted to share with others.

What is remarkable is that during this process, she continued her growth and went through more growing pains, both good and bad. She was able to maintain a positive perspective and strengths-based approach to the many changes that were happening in her life. During challenging times, I have been a part of Angelica's support system, and have been an ear to listen. Even as I was about to have a baby, I wanted to make sure that she was able to process her experience, and talk her through some of the most difficult decisions she has had to make. The bottom line for her has been to be authentic, and to make sure she has her children's best interest at heart.

While Angelica still faces many unknowns, I look forward to being a part of her constantly evolving life as she continues to reinvent herself.

Sophie E. Gavilanes
Professional School Counselor

ACKNOWLEDGEMENTS

To my parents, Guadalupe and Jose Robles, who came to the U.S. seeking the American dream, and through their struggles gave us the best life.

To my sister, Natalie, who has always been my protector and has shown me so much love and support.

To my brother, Eddie, who has always been there through the good and the bad. His sensible outlook and easiness to life are admirable.

To my dear sister, Liz, whom I love and adore. Thank you for opening your heart to me and allowing me to be part of your life.

To Ray, we created two gorgeous souls together and I am forever grateful for it.

To my lively, beautiful, athletic nieces and nephews Maya, Laila, Cooper, and Logan. Your happiness and joy for life is contagious.

To Lewis Senior for the foreword. You have played an integral role in my life, and I am forever grateful for your continued love and guidance.

To Sophie Gavilanes for the afterward. My dear amazing friend who has been by my side since we were eighteen years old, and built an incredible friendship throughout the years.

With my deepest affinity and appreciation to all of those who crossed my path in one way or another. You all have touched, moved, and inspired me. I am grateful to you all.

Gabrielle & Bill Baumeyer, Arturo Fuentes, Elnalyn Robles Costa, Natalie and Chris Fewell, Jennifer Perez, Jennifer Farina, Melanie Lewis, Boris Kasabov, Margot Katz, Danielle and Randy Doss, Monika Banach, Sonia Rash, Amanda Patrick, Muriel Flores, Becky and Jonathan Geck, Jasmine Ross, Steven Henriquez, Juan and Elsa Nieto, Claudia and Allen Saunders, Massiel Villegas, Jay Lyons, Michelle Velez, Devon Wade, Alida and Devin Brown, Ingrid Hillhouse, Dr. Rosalinda Garza, Laura Senior, David Senior, Ben McMahon, Sarah Klawisky, Don Hutson, Chameka Scott, Violeta Maldonado Tohme, Luis Enrique Badillo, Brian Sebastian and Carl Russell, Carmen Rodriguez, Juana Badillo, Minerva Badillo, Victoria Ibanez, Lyndon Jones, Ana Norton, Brittnye Shaffer, Anh Pham, Lee Perez, Makyba Lyons, Shannon McMillan Hernandez, Julie Bezerra, Lauren Stogner, Frank Guerrero, Veronica Solano, Oliver Mendoza, Hebert Del Villar, Buck Worley, Will O'Brien, Grant Roberts, Darrell Bolden, Aaron and Bekah Palaian, Thomas Hayden, Penny Dalfrey, Angelica Meals, Julie Hall, Jen Lee, Anibal Gutierrez, Lilly Gallegos, Magaly Alonzo, Raymond Martinez, Antonio and Verenice Escareno, Cindy Miranda, Maritza Hernandez, Beverly Roethke, Gail Benes, Arlene Watson, Missy Holtrup, Ana Eliopoulos, Randy Beckman, Angie Parker, Claudia Pineda, Jose Pereira, Mark and Emma Wilkinson, Rev. Rebecca Wilson, Jose Tapia, Roberto Castellanos, James Tapia, Juan Ortega Jr., Carolina Cartens, Cindy Santino, Gohar Firozgary, Claudia Bravo, Francis Leal, Tremaine Joseph, Dr. Julia Ward, Karen Looney, Rosie Munive, Ed Stanley, and RPC.

ABOUT THE AUTHOR

Angelica is the founder, owner and President of Adevar Investigative Group, a firm that specializes in providing case evaluation, suspect interrogation, victim and witness interviewing, expert witness services, and evidence and investigation summaries.

She has worked as a forensic investigator, interrogator, case manager and communication coach. She specializes in criminal Interviewing and Interrogation at the federal level. She has over 15 years of experience working with government investigations, corporate fraud, private investigations, youth in at-risk environments, adolescents, adults and criminals with mental illness.

Angelica is passionate about helping and empowering those around her. She has volunteered with non-profits and served as a leader for a fundraising team for the last 10 years, raising over a total of $120,000. She is an avid triathlete, trail runner and body builder, completing two Ironmans and well over 40 running and triathlon races. She is also a Wellness NPC Fitness competitor placed athlete.

After a year of creating beautiful balloon arrangements for her children's parties, and for her family and friends, Angelica decided to launch her second business, Angel Creations. She is self-taught and creating ballon decorations brings her solace, peace and joy. Angelica creates to inspire others to live a life they love. Her children are her biggest motivators and she is raising them to live a life without limits. Being a mother and a CEO of two successful businesses has been her greatest joy.

Angelica Robles Author & Speaker

If you have any questions about my debut book **Through These Brown Eyes**, would like to request an interview or enquire about a keynote speech or talk, please contact me through my website or social media platforms.

I look forward to hearing from you.

www.angelicaroblesofficial.com

www.instagram.com/Angelicarobles28

www.facebook.com/Adevar2017

www.linkedin.com/in/angelicarobleslopez

CHERISH OUR CHILDREN INC

More than 5 million children in America have watched their mothers or fathers go to prison.

Cherish Our Children International is dedicated to helping children of incarcerated parents.

DONATE

by visiting: www.cherishourchildren.org

HEARTS to be HEARD

Giving a Voice to Creativity!

With every donation, a voice will be given to the creativity that lies within the hearts of our children living with diverse challenges.

By making this difference, children that may not have been given the opportunity to have their Heart Heard will have the freedom to create beautiful works of art and musical creations.

Donate by visiting

HeartstobeHeard.com

We thank you.

Made in the USA
Coppell, TX
10 November 2021